**A CO-PRODUCTION BETWEEN
THE ROYAL LYCEUM THEATRE AND MALMÖ STADSTEATER**

TWO SISTERS

Written by David Greig
Directed by Wils Wilson

Two Sisters was first performed at the Royal Lyceum Theatre
on Saturday 10th February 2024

TWO SISTERS

by David Greig

Cast

in alphabetical order

Emma	**Jessica Hardwick**
Amy	**Shauna Macdonald**
Lance	**Erik Olsson**

Chorus

Nicola Anderson
Sam Barclay
Kasper Borycki
Ciara Browning
Amie Bryson
Hector R. J.
  Buchanan
Ben Carroll
Aaron Chilton-Kidd
Jack Clark
Josh Clunie
Amy Craik
Skie Mathieson
  Dobie
Jessica Donaldson
Océane Doppel

Shadi El-Dah
Matthew
  Fotheringham
Josh Gately
Ella Greenhill
Mia Haden
Jack Harrison
Gabrielle Henderson
Jack Houliston
Ellie Hunter
Iga Kurpik
Ivy
Cameron Leonard
Nualla Macgregor
Grace Marshall
Meghan Mathews

Niall McCluskey
Zack McGlynn
Kieran McKeown
Aidan McKinlay
Ruby Muldownie
Jack Nisbet
Lucia Demitri Von
  Pezold
Chelsea Quaison
Emily Reid
Remo Santangeli
Gregor Shanley
Dorian Todd
Charlie Watt
Lucy West
Hannah Wilson

Creative Team

Writer	**David Greig**
Director	**Wils Wilson**
Designer	**Lisbeth Burian**
Movement & Intimacy Director	**Janice Parker**
Lighting Designer	**Colin Grenfell**
Composer & Sound Designer	**MJ McCarthy**
Fight Director	**EmmaClaire Brightlyn**
Costume Supervisor	**Sophie Ferguson**
Associate Director	**André Agius**
Chorus Coordinator	**Debi Pirie**
Stage Manager	**Lee Davis**
Deputy Stage Manager	**Chariya Glasse-Davies**
Assistant Stage Manager	**Millie Jones**
Creative Learning Producer	**Kerrie Walker**
Producer	**David Dey**

CAST

EMMA | JESSICA HARDWICK

Lyceum Credits: *Rhinoceros, Crime and Punishment* (Citizens Theatre, Royal Lyceum Theatre), *The Venetian Twins.*

Recent Theatre Credits: *The Comedy of Errors* (Citizens Theatre); *Meet Me at Dawn* (Arcola Theatre); *Cyrano de Bergerac, The Strange Undoing of Prudencia Hart* (National Theatre of Scotland); *Knives in Hens* (Perth Theatre); *The Rivals* (Bristol Old Vic); *Lanark: A Life in Three Acts* (Edinburgh International Festival & Citizens Theatre).

TV & Film: *Float* (BBC/Canal+; Best Short Series (Series Mania, France) and Best Scripted Drama (RTS Scotland))*; Shetland* (BBC); *Annika* (Alibi); *Six Four* (ITV/House productions); *Payback* (ITV/Britbox); *The Lost King* (Baby Cow/BBC Films).

Awards: CATS Best Actress nomination (*Cyrano de Bergerac*); CATS Winner Best Actress (*Knives in Hens*).

AMY | SHAUNA MACDONALD

Lyceum Credits: *Victory, Mary Queen of Scots Got Her Head Chopped Off.*

Recent Theatre Credits: *Mouthpiece, Born to Run* (Traverse Theatre); *King Lear* (Citizens Theatre); *Realism* (National Theatre of Scotland); *A View From the Bridge* (Birmingham Rep/West Yorkshire Playhouse); *Pal Joey* (Citizens Theatre); *The Home Project* (National Theatre).

TV, Film & Radio: Television: *Mayflies, Shetland S6, The Scotts, Danger Mouse, Outlander, The Nest, Liar, In Plain Sight, Hold the Sunset, The Cry, Ransom, The Catchment, The Five, Murder, Katie Morag, Waterloo Road, Ripper Street, Case Histories, Bonekickers, Sea of Souls, Spooks, State of Play, Taggart, Wedding Belles.* Film: *Balance not Symmetry, White Chamber, Star Wars Episode VII: The Last Jedi, Nails, Moondogs, Soldier Bee, The Correspondence, Howl, Swung, Made in Belfast, Filth, The Hike, The Descent II, The Mutant Chronicles, Jetsam, The Descent, Niceland, The Rocket Post, Late Night Shopping, Daybreak, The Debt Collector.* Radio: *Tenderness of Boys, This Thing of Darkness, Off Grid, When the Pips Stop, The Poet and the Echo, Falling, Rebus: The Black Book*

Awards: Best Actress, RTS award (*The Scotts*); Best Actress, BAFTA (*White Chamber*); Best Actress, The Stage Edinburgh (*Mouthpiece*)

LANCE | ERIK OLSSON

Recent Theatre Credits: Erik Olsson has worked as an actor at Malmö Stadsteater since 2005, in more than 50 plays, including *The World is Full of Married Men, De Skamlösa, Tears of Malmö, En midsommarnattsdröm, Hedda Gabler, Halva Månen, Cheffen, Måsen, Kejsarens Nya Kläder, En Handelsresandes Död, De Skyddssökande Kvinnorna.*

Film: *Skulden, Arvet, Four Women*

CREATIVE TEAM

WRITER | DAVID GREIG

Lyceum Credits: *Group Portrait in a Summer Landscape* (Director), *The Strange Undoing of Prudencia Hart, Solaris, Local Hero, Touching the Void, Creditors, The Suppliant Women.*

Recent Theatre Credits: *Local Hero* (Minerva Theatre); *Adventures with the Painted People, Under Another Sky* (Pitlochry Festival Theatre); *Charlie and the Chocolate Factory, The Lorax* (The Old Vic); *The Events* (Young Vic); *The Strange Undoing of Prudencia Hart* (National Theatre of Scotland); *Dunsinane* (Hampstead Theatre and tour); *Midsummer* (Traverse Theatre and tour).

David Greig is a multi-award-winning playwright who became the Artistic Director of the Royal Lyceum Edinburgh in 2015.

DIRECTOR | WILS WILSON

Lyceum Credits: *Life is a Dream, Red Ellen* (Lyceum/Northern Stage/Nottingham Playhouse), *Twelfth Night* (Lyceum/Bristol Old Vic), *The Hour We Knew Nothing of Each Other, Cockpit, Wind Resistance* (Lyceum/Edinburgh International Festival).

Recent Theatre Credits: *Macbeth* (Royal Shakespeare Company); *The Strange Undoing of Prudencia Hart* (Double M Productions/Lyceum/National Theatre of Scotland); *I Want My Hat Back* (National Theatre); *The 306 Dusk* (National Theatre of Scotland/Perth); *Candylion, Praxis Makes Perfect* (National Theatre Wales); *Gastronauts* (Royal Court).

Television, Film & Radio: Audio: *Portal* (Lepus Productions); Short Film: *CROWD* (ghostbag).

Awards: Awards include Drama Desk, Herald Angel and CATS Awards (*The Strange Undoing of Prudencia Hart*); Best Director CATS Awards (*Life is a Dream*); and Welsh Theatre Awards (*Praxis Makes Perfect*); Manchester Evening News Theatre Award (*Of Mice and Men*); nominations for Olivier Award (*I Want My Hat Back*) and UK Theatre Awards (*Life is a Dream, Manchester Lines*).

DESIGNER | LISBETH BURIAN

Recent Theatre Credits: *Arendt – Seeing in the Dark, Building a Road, The Man Without a Past* (Odense Teater); *The Face of Evil, Inga and Lutz* (Svalegangen Theater); *Pigion Superstition* (Pavillion Vvillette); *Monica's Wals* (Malmö Stadsteater); *Pelle the Conqueror:* Artmovie/performance, *Obsessed* (Bornholms Teater); *Last Christmas* (Odsherred Teater); *Asta* (The Floting Theater); *Stand Firm* (The Royal Theater, Denmark); *Without* (Husets Teater).

Awards: Best Eksperimentel Production (*Hair on it*).

Training: Académi du Viaduc des Beaux-Arts, Paris, The National School of Performing Arts, Set & Costume Design & Master in Design – Sustainability, Leadership and Design, Copenhagen.

MOVEMENT & INTIMACY DIRECTOR | JANICE PARKER

Lyceum Credits: *Castle Lennox* (Lung Ha/The Lyceum); *The Strange Undoing of Prudencia Hart, Life Is a Dream, The Hour We Knew Nothing of Each Other, Glory on Earth.*

Recent Theatre Credits: *Medea* (Edinburgh International Festival/National Theatre of Scotland); *Wind Resistance* (Karine Polwart); *The View from Castle Rock, Age of Arousal, The Girls of Slender Means* (Stellar Quines); *Crazy Jane* (Birds of Paradise); *Exotic Hyper Space, Instant Travel to Pop Up Cities* (Lung Ha).

Recent Dance Credits: *To Avoid Falling Apart* (The Travelling Gallery); *Not Brittle, Not Rigid, Not Fixed* (Edinburgh Art Festival); *Small Acts of Hope and Lament* (Edinburgh International Festival); *Writing The Body* (National Galleries of Scotland); *Glory, What Would Richard Do?, You Said You Liked The Dancing, Private Dancer* (Janice Parker Projects); *The Living Room Dances* (The Albert Drive Project).

Awards: *Herald Angel, Creative Scotland Award, Saltire Society Outstanding Woman of Scotland.*

LIGHTING DESIGNER | COLIN GRENFELL

Lyceum Credits: *The Beauty Queen of Leenane, Christmas Dinner.*

Recent Theatre Credits: *Medea, Black Watch, The Bacchae, 365, Men Should Weep* (NTS); *Tamburlaine* (RSC); *Theatre of Blood, Lifegame, Lost Without Words* (National Theatre); *Pride and Prejudice* (*sort of)* (West End & Touring); *70 Hill Lane, Tao of Glass, The Hanging Man, Coma, Spirit, Still No Idea* (Improbable); *Adults, Still, This is Paradise, The Devil Masters, Pandas* (Traverse); *The Mother, The Mentor, A Midsummer Night's Dream* (Theatre Royal Bath); *Pirates of Penzance* (Scottish Opera); *The Caretaker* (West End, International Tour); *The Cherry Orchard, Kes, Macbeth, Gypsy, Separate Tables* (Manchester Royal Exchange); *Wolfie* (Tron Theatre); *The King of Hell's Palace* (Hampstead Theatre); *Macbeth, Tartuffe, Canary* (Liverpool Everyman & Playhouse).

Television, Film & Radio: 6 Christmas specials for Cbeebies.

Awards: CATS Best Design (*Elephant Man*); Theatre Wales Awards (*Cat on a Hot Tin Roof*, Theatre Clwyd); TMA Best Design (*Hanging Man*).

COMPOSER & SOUND DESIGNER | MJ MCCARTHY

Lyceum Credits: *Castle Lennox, Lyceum Christmas Tales, Pride & Prejudice* (*sort of), The Duchess (of Malfi), Wendy & Peter Pan, The Hour We Knew Nothing of Each Other, Glory on Earth, The Weir, Bondagers.*

Recent Theatre Credits: *The Fair Maid of the West* (Royal Shakespeare Company); *The Grand Old Opera House Hotel* (Traverse Theatre); *England & Son, Tin Cat* (HOME Manchester); *Kidnapped* (National Theatre of Scotland); *Red Riding Hood* (Citizens Theatre); *Cinderella* (Dundee Rep); *The Last Return* (Druid Theatre Company); *The Strange Undoing of Prudencia Hart* (Manchester Royal Exchange); *Pride & Prejudice* (*sort of)* (Criterion Theatre); *Nora: A Doll's House* (Young Vic & Citizens Theatre); *Whatever Happened to the Jaggy Nettles?* (Citizens Theatre); *I Can Go Anywhere* (Traverse Theatre); *Tay Bridge* (Dundee Rep).

Television, Film & Radio: *Hey! Ronnie Reagan, Pitching Up, Where You're Meant to Be* (Film) *On the Hemline* (TV).

FIGHT DIRECTOR | EMMACLAIRE BRIGHTLYN

Lyceum Credits: *The Snow Queen, Pride and Prejudice** (**sort of*), *Twelfth Night, Cockpit.*

Recent Theatre Credits: *Adults, Crocodile Fever, Ulster American* (Traverse Theatre); *Lear's Fool, Julius Caesar, Jekyll and Hyde, Much Ado About Nothing, The Tempest, Queen Lear, Measure for Measure, Taming of the Shrew, Timon of Athens* (Bard in the Botanics); *The Children, All My Sons, Gagarin Way, August: Osage County* (Dundee Rep Theatre); *Dracula: Mina's Reckoning, The Panopticon, Dragon* (National Theatre of Scotland); *Stuntman* (Superfan); *Private Lives* (Pitlochry Festival Theatre); *Don Juan, Richard III, Knives in Hens* (Perth Theatre); *The Dodo Experiment, This Restless House Trilogy, Dance of Death* (Citz Theatre); *Romeo and Juliet* (Cumbernauld Theatre); *Eat Me* (Snap-Elastic); *Stornoway Quebec* (Theatre Gu Leor).

Television, Film & Radio: Short Films: *Mother Daughter, Broono, Chrysalis, The Difference Between Us*. Feature Films: *BEATS, Anna and the Apocalypse*. TV: *Demon Headmaster.*

Previous Artistic Director of The International Order of the Sword and the Pen.

ASSOCIATE DIRECTOR | ANDRÉ AGIUS

Lyceum Credits: *Wonder Festival* (Assistant Producer).

Recent Theatre Credits: *Impromptu at Òran Mór, Davina & Goliath, The Words, The Infernal Serpent* (A Play a Pie and a Pint); *Utter Filth* (Traverse Theatre & Performing Arts Studio Scotland); *Scotland Through Time* (Edinburgh International Book Festival); *Ding Dong Dash!* (Babel International Performing Arts Festival, Romania); *The Hothouse* (*Is-Serra*) (Teatru Malta, Malta's National Theatre Company); *Peer Gynt* (Malta's National Philharmonic Orchestra); *ŻfinMade* (ŻfinMalta, Malta's National Dance Company); *Skylight* (MADC); *Decameron* (Teatru Manoel, The National Theatre of Malta); *DripFeed* (Studio18 Malta); *Kantilena* (Sharjah Heritage Days Dubai); *The Rose Tattoo* (The English Theatre of Frankfurt); *A Year and A Day* (Arcola Theatre).

Television, Film & Radio: *The Dovekeepers* (TV), *You, Me and the Apocalypse* (TV), *The Devils Double* (Film), *BBC's The Whale* (TV), Agora (Film); *13 hours: The Secret Soldiers of Benghazi* (Film), *Paul, Apostle of Christ* (Film), *Largo Winch* (Film).

THEATRE MADE IN EDINBURGH

ARTISTIC DIRECTOR **DAVID GREIG**
EXECUTIVE DIRECTOR **MIKE GRIFFITHS**

The Royal Lyceum Theatre Edinburgh is the leading producing theatre in Scotland and one of the United Kingdom's most prolific theatre companies.

The Royal Lyceum Theatre Edinburgh sits at the heart of the city in our 140-year-old building, welcoming over 100,000 people each year.

At the Lyceum, we believe that theatre is good for the soul. Led by our Artistic Director David Greig, we bring the best theatre from around the world to Edinburgh and share the best of Scottish theatre with the world.

We're experts in making theatre. We rehearse in our studio space across the road from the auditorium, and our costumes and sets are designed and built in house at our workshop in Roseburn, Edinburgh.

Community is at the heart of what we do. In 2024, our creative learning department celebrates twenty-five years of developing and nurturing talent. Our Youth Theatre programmes have been the starting point for many Scottish actors, fostering newfound confidence and lifelong friendships. We also host sixty-plus writing groups, technical courses and training.

Over the past fifty-nine years the Lyceum has continued to make world-class theatre – take a seat, and experience it for yourself.

For the latest information about The Lyceum visit **lyceum.org.uk**

ALBA | CHRUTHACHAIL

Two Sisters

David Greig is a writer and theatre director. He was born in Edinburgh in 1969. His play *Europe* was performed at the Traverse Theatre in 1994. Since then, his plays, adaptations and musical scripts have been performed widely in the UK and around the world. In 1990 he co-founded Suspect Culture, who produced collaborative, experimental work until their funding was ended in 2010. In 2016 he became the Artistic Director of Edinburgh's Royal Lyceum Theatre. In 2023 he published his first novel, *Columba's Bones*.

DAVID GREIG

Two Sisters

faber

First published in 2024
by Faber and Faber Limited
The Bindery, 51 Hatton Garden,
London, EC1N 8HN

Typeset by Brighton Gray
Printed and bound in the UK by CPI Group (Ltd), Croydon CR0 4YY

David Greig is hereby identified as author
of this work in accordance with Section 77 of the
Copyright, Designs and Patents Act 1988

A CIP record for this book
is available from the British Library

ISBN 978-0-571-38898-1

Printed and bound in the UK on FSC® certified paper in line with our contin
commitment to ethical business practices, sustainability and the environr

2 4 6 8 10 9 7 5 3 1

Acknowledgements

Two Sisters would not exist without the persistence of four brilliant theatre directors.

In 2014, my friend, then director of Actors Touring Company, Ramin Gray, had suggested we make a play with a chorus of young people. He arranged a workshop with the Unicorn Theatre in London. For months I was unable to write. Finally, on the last morning of the workshop, desperate and hungover, I sat in Costa Coffee and wrote a scene. That scene turned out to be the opening scene. Later that morning, Ramin noted that I had written this in Times New Roman rather than Helvetica, the choice for all my previous work. 'This is good, David,' he said, 'you're writing in a new font.'

Ramin's encouragement sparked a flame that burned, sputtered, guttered and faded to barely an ember when, in 2019, it was picked up by Ella Caldwell, the Artistic Director of Red Stitch Theatre Company in Melbourne. Ella asked if I had any new stuff. I said that running a theatre had got in the way, but I had some fragments and sent her a document. The next day she told me she loved it and I had to finish the story. She organised a series of readings with Red Stitch and State Arts of Geelong.

Then there was a pandemic.

I showed the script to Kitte Wagner, the Artistic Director of Malmö Stadsteater. The play reminded her of her own sibling relationship – she didn't say whether she was Emma or Amy – and she knew exactly who should play Lance. She arranged a Zoom reading and we agreed to co-produce.

Finally, as the virus ebbed, the dramaturgical baton was picked up by Lyceum Associate Wils Wilson, and she has brought the play to the stage some ten years after I wrote that first scene.

I want to thank Ramin, Ella, Kitte and Wils for their care and determination in pushing me to bring *Two Sisters* into being.

I would like to thank all the actors and young people in Edinburgh, London, Melbourne and Malmö who have workshopped *Two Sisters* and helped it find its form. In particular, Amanda Drew, Amanda Hale, Alan Williams; the actors of the Red Stitch Ensemble; the actors of the Malmö Stadsteater Ensemble, the young people from Unicorn Theatre, Stage Arts Geelong, Lyceum Youth Theatre, the drama students of Fife College and the drama students of Edinburgh College. Also, thanks to Stephen and the team at Pettycur Bay Holiday Park for their insights and guided tours.

Two Sisters was first performed at the Royal Lyceum Theatre, Edinburgh, on 10 February 2024, with the following cast:

Emma Jessica Hardwick
Amy Shauna Macdonald
Lance Erik Olsson
Chorus Nicola Anderson, Sam Barclay, Kasper Borycki, Ciara Browning, Amie Bryson, Hector R. J. Buchanan, Ben Carroll, Aaron Chilton-Kidd, Jack Clark, Josh Clunie, Amy Craik, Skie Mathieson Dobie, Jessica Donaldson, Océane Doppel, Shadi El-Dah, Matthew Fotheringham, Josh Gately, Ella Greenhill, Mia Haden, Jack Harrison, Gabrielle Henderson, Jack Houliston, Ellie Hunter, Iga Kurpik, Ivy, Cameron Leonard, Nualla Macgregor, Grace Marshall, Meghan Mathews, Niall McCluskey, Zack McGlynn, Kieran McKeown, Aidan McKinlay, Ruby Muldownie, Jack Nisbet, Lucia Demitri Von Pezold, Chelsea Quaison, Emily Reid, Remo Santangeli, Gregor Shanley, Dorian Todd, Charlie Watt, Lucy West, Hannah Wilson

Director Wils Wilson
Designer Lisbeth Burian
Movement and Intimacy Director Janice Parker
Lighting Designer Colin Grenfell
Composer and Sound Designer MJ McCarthy
Fight Director EmmaClaire Brightlyn
Costume Supervisor Sophie Ferguson
Associate Director André Agius
Chorus Coordinator Debi Pirie
Stage Manager Lee Davis
Deputy Stage Manager Chariya Glasse-Davies
Assistant Stage Manager Millie Jones
Creative Learning Producer Kerrie Walker
Producer David Dey

Characters

Amy

Emma

Lance

The Kids

Setting

A holiday caravan park on the coast.

Some time around the year 2010.

TWO SISTERS

A Note on the Kids Chorus

Two Sisters is written to be performed with a chorus of teenagers: The Kids.

The Kids should be an existing youth group, or youth theatre group, or school group. It is very important that they should not be 'cast' from auditions. Any kid who is part of the group and who wants to take part in the play should be able to have a role.

During any individual run of the play it's possible to have a number of different Kids choruses taking part on different nights. The 'feel' of the play should be that the Kids are themselves, not characters, and that their individuality is part of creating the stage atmosphere.

The Kids are sometimes assigned dialogue. This is indicated by a dash and dialogue written in italics. This dialogue can be assigned to appropriate kids as best fits whichever group is involved.

Kid A and Kid B have dramatic roles at a key moment in the play. They should be rehearsed and practise separately.

The Kids also have a choric function. The choruses are made of material gathered from the audience who will have answered 'The Summer Special Questionnaire'. The Associate Director or Stage Manager on the night should choose which audience answers will be read out. Answers should be chosen randomly, eliminating only unreadable ones or any which are in some way rude or unpleasant.

In general, the play is constructed so that any person's answer should work.

There are many ways to gather audience answers to the Summer Special Questionnaire. They could be filled out online, by a smartphone app, or questionnaires might be put in the programme.

Before the play begins, the Kids should go on stage and should guide the audience through the questions. This way the audience will share a collective experience of remembering what it was like to be sixteen.

Once the answers are received, they can be distributed to the Kids before each act.

It's okay for the Kids to hold the written answers in their hands. We should know they are reading and reacting to these texts for the first time.

Lastly, during rehearsal, the Kids should choose a song which is to be their own special summer song. Perhaps they will vote on it, perhaps it will be obvious, but it will belong entirely to them. That song features at a couple of moments in the play.

If you are reading the play, it might be fun for you to complete the questionnaire before you read it, then you can imagine your answers being read out at the appropriate moments.

In this text, the chorus answers are taken from a 2019 workshop with the actors of the Red Stitch Theatre Company in Melbourne.

Summer Special Questionnaire

Remember the summer you were sixteen years old. Close your eyes. Transport yourself back in time. Perhaps you are on holiday? Perhaps just at home but not in school? What year is it? What music is on the radio? Where do you live? What is happening in your life?

Think of one particular moment, it doesn't matter which one, just a moment that seems typical of the time . . . Now answer these questions:

1. *Where are you? What is the weather like? What are you doing?*

2. *What's alive in your heart, and why?*

3. *What clothes are you wearing?*

4. *Who is your crush, and why?*

5. *What is your favourite going-out song right now?*

6. *How do you dance?*

7. *Imagine your sixteen-year-old self could see you as you are now. What three questions would young you ask old you about their future?*

8. *Please answer your sixteen-year-old's questions truthfully.*

Act One

Holiday Heaven.
 Friday afternoon.
 Heat, sun.

We are outside a static holiday caravan on the edge of a park.
 The caravan has a little 'stoop' area outside the front door with two plastic chairs.
 Nearby there's a play park. Perhaps it has a climbing frame or a swing, perhaps a roundabout but, whatever play equipment is there, there's not much and it's old.
 The day's too hot for any great excitement anyway.
 A moment.
 Amy enters, dressed for the city, wearing sunglasses, carrying a polythene bag.
 She checks the nameplate on the caravan, tries the door handle. It doesn't open. She tries again. Still no luck. Fuck it.
 She takes a bottle of sparkling wine out of the polythene bag.
 She carefully pops the cork, pours some into a plastic cup, lights a cigarette.
 And drinks.
 The Kids enter.
 They arrange themselves around the play park.
 They read out the audience's answers to the first question.

Kids It's summer, you're sixteen, describe the scene.

— 1975, in a beautiful huge, old home with a ballroom. The sun is shining.

— 1984, in the backyard of my parents' (family) home. It's night. It's cold, cooler than we think it is. I'm drinking bad vodka and Mountain Dew with my friends. There's a bonfire.

— 1990, at my friend Simon's listening to his brother's Nirvana album, *Bleach*.

— 1982, in one of the music-lesson rooms at school when we should be in a class.

— 1984, it's raining, lashing on the windows, we are in the projections room in the school library. We are making too much noise. Mr Librarian open-heartedly tells us off for the hundredth time.

— 1980, on a BMX track. It's gloomy with a slight chill in the air. I'm riding my green mountain bike.

— 2000, in my boyfriend's house in the pool. It's a hot afternoon.

— 1976, at my friend Stevie's house. It's hot. We are tie-dyeing clothes from the op shop – slips and things. And going to the creek.

— 1980, in my friend's backyard sitting around the table, drinking and laughing while listening to music. It's sunny and warm with a slight breeze.

Kids What's alive in your heart, and why?

— The Cure, schoolyards, trying cigarettes and beer, history assignments.

— I'm fantasising about my next-door neighbour.

— A seminal nineties computer game (Populous), staying up late, sneaking Bundaberg rum shots, maybe a little hard-copy porn.

— An awakened sense of creativity.

— My girlfriend's being a haven.

— I feel potential, excitement, the world beckons, power.

— I'm twitching to get out of my country town and into the world. Like a bull at the gate. I'm also anxious.

— Showing off being clever and not being afraid of it.

— The feeling that these are the best days of our lives (oh, how naive).

They have finished the audience questions.

Kids Shall we start?

They agree to start.

It's summer, it's 2010, it's a holiday park on the coast, the sort of place people come to every year . . . it's hot and some kids are . . . I don't know . . .

Just mooching about I guess.

Emma enters, dressed for leisure, just noticeably pregnant, pulling a smart wheelie suitcase and carrying a large smart leather bag over her shoulder.
As she walks, she talks into her headphones.

Emma Fine . . .

. . .

Campsite's fine, journey was good, car was good, it's all fine.

. . .

No, tell Dan, I haven't seen Amy.

. . .

I don't know where she is.

. . .

Well, if she calls I won't know, will I, because I'm on retreat, remember?

. . .

Okay. Okay, fine.

. . .

I'm switching off now, love. I'm switching off for the
week . . . I love you . . . love you . . .

. . .

Okay.

. . .

. . . love you . . . bye bye bye bye bye.

Emma ends the call.
  Switches her phone off.
  And puts her phone away.
  Amy gives her a look.

Emma What?

Amy 'Love you . . . bye bye bye.'

Amy mimes puking.

Emma You should be grateful I didn't tell on you.

Emma looks at the caravan.
  A moment.

Is this Paradise?

Amy Holiday Heaven.

Emma Did you see the 'For Sale' sign.

Amy Sad.

Emma I remember it all being brighter, somehow.

Emma tries the door.

Amy It's locked.

Emma Didn't the lady give you the key?

Amy The caretaker has to check everything's okay.

Emma Is there some doubt about everything being okay?

Amy It hasn't been occupied since last summer. There
might be spiders.

Emma I booked it months ago.

Amy You booked Nirvana. Nirvana's a single. Paradise is a twin.

Emma I don't need a twin.

Amy I do.

Emma You're not staying.

Amy Come on, sis.

Emma Get your own caravan.

Amy I've already paid the difference.
Besides, Paradise has a balconette.

Emma This place is not like I remember it.

Emma What are we supposed to do until the caretaker comes?

Amy 'Relax . . .'

Emma sits.

'. . . and watch the majestic play of dappled light on water.'

Amy reads from the camp brochure.

'Welcome to Holiday Heaven Holiday Park. All our caravans are fitted to the highest standards, complete with hot and cold running water, fully equipped kitchen area, microwave, en suite, shower, and a complimentary outdoor barbecue.
'In addition, our "Paradise", "Olympus" and "Valhalla" lodges are blessed with a roomy balconette upon which we invite you to relax and watch the majestic play of dappled light on water.'

Emma All I can see is kids. It's menacing.

Amy They're just mooching. We were the same when we were their age.

Emma No, we weren't.

Amy Remember all those afternoons, bored out of our tiny minds.

Emma I wasn't bored.

A moment.

Amy Look at the gulls.
The way they fly against the buffets.
Around – up – down – around – up – down.
Their little hearts bursting against the wind.
It must be very tiring.
Fighting just to stand still.
It's quite moving.
I think it's quite moving.
Don't you think it's quite moving?

Emma Not really.
They're rats.

Amy Maybe they like the wind.
Maybe the wind helps them hover over the bins.

A moment.

Emma Amy, you need to go home.

Amy I can't go home.

Emma Well, you can't stay here.

Amy Why not?

Emma I'm writing. I'm on a retreat.

Amy You're a lawyer, Emma, it's a fucking holiday.

Emma People write, Amy, even lawyers.
Books.
They don't come from nowhere. People write them. And, in order to write them, they go on retreat.

Amy Are you writing a book?

Emma Maybe.

Amy What sort of book?

Emma A novel.
Or maybe a novella.
Or maybe a series of interlinked short stories.
I can't quite decide.

Amy What's it about?

Emma A woman.
An ordinary woman.
Except she's not ordinary, because nobody is ordinary really.
But you know she's just like you or me except.
She's caught up in World War Two France.
Her husband's in the Resistance.
But she ends up sheltering a wounded German soldier.
And she falls in love with him but –
Then the whole village gets burned down and they have to go on the run.

Amy What's her name? This scarlet *traîtresse*? This French tart?

Emma I haven't decided yet.

Amy Marie-Claire?
Genevieve?
Emma?

Emma Amy, why do you have to be so –

Amy What?

Emma Why do you always have to piss on my parade.

Amy I'm not pissing on your parade.

Emma You are.

Amy Is there a parade?

Emma You know what I mean.

A moment.

Amy Please let me stay.

Emma I need space.

Amy You need company, trust me, writing's boring.
You'll just spend the day wanking and eating toast.

Emma You are disgusting.

Amy I know, I'm sorry.
I'll help you write.

Emma How?

Amy I'll bring you lunch.

Emma I don't want lunch.

Amy I'll type.

Emma No.

Amy I'll proofread.
I'll research.
I'll massage your shoulders.

Emma Amy, I'm trying to explore my creativity!
It's not fair to – just because you –

Amy Because I what –?

Emma Nothing.
The whole idea of this trip is for me to finally realise my creative potential before the baby comes and I just become a mum.

A moment.

Amy Baby's ages away.
You hardly look pregnant at all.

Not even plump.
You look hot in fact.
You could pull.
We could pull.
We could pull tonight if you like.
Go to a nightclub.
Country town.
Realise some creative potential.

Emma No.

Amy Emma, where else am I supposed to go?

Emma Stay with a friend.

Amy I don't have a friend.
Not like you.
Not family.
Not someone who'll take me when I'm in disgrace.
Please, just for the weekend, till Dan calms down, and then I'll go home, I promise.
Please?

A moment.

Emma You always do this. You always do it. You're like –

Amy What?

A moment.

Emma You're like that red plastic mesh they use to fence off roadworks in the street.

Amy What?

Emma You're everywhere! Blocking me off. Hemming me in. I can't go where I want to go – do what I want to do – and then, one day, just when I manage to get away to the seaside, to find some peace and quiet on my own, in nature, here you are again – a great big tangled-up mess of crappy plastic washed up on the beach.

Amy That is a somewhat rococo metaphor.

Emma Fuck you.

A moment.

Amy I just need a bed, sis.

A moment.

Emma Have you thought about getting help?

Amy What sort of help?

Emma Therapy.

Amy I thought about it, but I realised it would take so long to explain the problem I'd get bored before we'd even started.

Emma That's not how therapy works.

Amy Isn't it?

Emma No.

Amy How would you know?

Emma Because I've done it.

Amy You've been in therapy?

Emma Yes.

Amy There's nothing wrong with you.

Emma You don't have to have something wrong with you to be in therapy.
It's just a good thing to do.
Like going to the gym.
You should try it.

Amy It's fine.
I just have to avoid being alone.

A moment.

Emma Why did Dan throw you out?

Amy He didn't throw me out. I walked out.

Emma Was it the affair?

A moment.

Amy Zz.

Emma Zz?

Amy Affairzz. It was the affairzz.

Emma Oh.

Amy . . .

Emma How many?

Amy Does it matter?

Emma I'm curious.

Amy I'm not even sure you could call them affairs. 'Affairs'. It's such a ridiculous word. It's so . . . Noël Coward. Oh Camilla. Oh Sebastian. Must we always meet in Didcot? Darling, we must, for we are having an 'affair'.

Emma How many?

Amy Are you jealous?

Emma How many?

Amy In all? Or merely during the relevant period?

Emma . . .

Amy A lot.

Emma . . .

Amy About six during the relevant period.

Emma . . .

Amy Of which details have recently emerged about three.

Emma Emerged?

Amy He hacked my phone. Which he had no right to do, by the way. It was a complete invasion of privacy.

Emma Hacked?

Amy Looked at.

Emma What made him suspicious?

Amy He came home and found me fucking the plumber.

Emma The plumber?

Amy In the kids' bed.
I say plumber, technically he's a heating engineer.
Roberto.

Emma Is that really his name?

Amy As far as I know.

Emma As far as you know?

Amy We're not close.
He was only there to fix the boiler.

Emma Roberto the plumber?

Amy I'm perfectly aware of the cliché. You don't need to drive the point home.

Emma What were you thinking?

Amy Not much.
It's not a thoughtful process, adultery.
One doesn't plan it –

Emma Doesn't one?

Amy No.

Emma So, it was all just a big accident?
Six affairs.
In the relevant period.
Adultery just happened to you?

Amy I didn't seek it out.

Emma But, nevertheless, you found it.

Amy I made myself available to it as a possibility.

Emma How?

A moment.

Amy What do you mean, how?

Emma How did you know it was possible?
With Roberto?

Amy I don't know.
Awareness.
Movement.
Glances.

Emma . . .

Amy . . .

Emma Ugh.

Amy What!?

Emma It's all so animal.
Physical.
I mean it's so – so – so – it's like *shitting.*
Or pissing . . . you have a need and you seek relief.
Base.

Amy It's not like that for me.

Emma Really?

Amy Yes really.
Your evocative imagery doesn't quite capture my experience.

Emma Then what sort of imagery would capture your experience?

Amy You honestly want to know the truth?

Emma Why do you think I might not want to honestly know the truth?

Amy Because you don't like frailty in other humans.

Emma I see.

Amy And faced with frailty, you become afraid, and end up being judgemental.

Emma Do I?

Amy You do.

Emma Well, I didn't fuck a plumber in my kids' bed.
So.
You know.
Swings and roundabouts.

Amy . . .

Emma . . .

Amy See, that was quite judgemental.

Emma In your kids' bed, Amy, for fuck's sake!

A moment.

Amy We had a rule.

Emma What?

Amy Dan and I.
We had a rule.
No one else in the marital bed. The marital bed is sacrosanct.
So, by doing it in the bunk bed, I was – in my way – adhering to the code.

A moment.

Emma I mean I can't speak for Dan, but, as a lawyer,
I imagine the reason he didn't suggest an amendment to

your code about also not fucking in the kids' bed . . .
I imagine the reason he didn't append subclause B2
'Regarding the Sanctity of the Infants' Sleeping Places
also' . . . is because . . . is because . . . is because he never in
a million years thought you would be brazen enough to
actually do it.

Amy You're not Dan's lawyer.

Emma That's just as well.

Amy Why?

Emma Because if I was I'd take you to the cleaners.

A moment.

What position did you do it in?

Amy What position!?

Emma Were you on top, on all fours, what?

Amy It isn't really any of your business.

Emma I want to know.

Amy Is it important?

Emma Oddly yes.

Amy Conventional missionary, largely.

Emma Good.

Amy Why's that good?

Emma Because if I imagine you being on top looking down
at Roberto's no-doubt-unshaven Italianate face haloed by a
Barney the Dinosaur pillowcase and duvet I feel . . . sick.

Amy . . .

Emma I mean. I think if you could see that pillowcase and
not . . . pause . . . I would have to revise my opinion of you.

Amy Down?

Emma Yes, Amy, I would be revising it down.

Amy Goodness.

Only the tone of voice you've been using so far has given me the distinct sense there wasn't any more down left available to for me to fall, opinion-wise, from you. So . . . you know . . . in an odd way, I suppose . . . I'm mildly flattered.

Emma Don't be.

Amy Emma . . .

. . .

When I fuck.

. . .

It feels like – for a moment – for just a few moments – like I lose myself entirely in timelessness – it feels like spinning into a place where I'm both perfectly and completely and wholly present and also at the same time entirely apart . . . It feels as if – behind everything in the universe – behind all the mundane experience of daily life – washing dishes – working – ignoring each other – that behind all that there's another layer – a layer of existence that binds us all together – like magnetism – sky – earth – soul: a connecting realm.

In the moments of sex . . . in the glances, the movement, the possibility, the fucking . . . in those moments.

. . .

I find myself drawn to the connecting realm.

. . .

And once there, I lose myself.
I shatter.
And simultaneously I'm made whole.

. . .

Now, for you, that might be like 'shitting'.
For me it's something more complex.

Emma . . .

Amy . . .

Emma What was it like when Dan came in?

Amy Embarrassing.

Emma I bet.

Amy More embarrassing for Roberto.

Emma Why?

Amy Dan made him stay and finish.

Emma What?

Amy Well, the boiler was broken so we didn't have hot water and it's a pain getting a plumber at the best of times but on Easter weekend . . . so he was just being practical I suppose . . . which is very Dan.

Emma And what did you feel?

Amy What did I feel?

Emma Upon your return from the connecting realm?

Amy Relief.

Emma Relief?

Amy Like when a shoplifter finally gets caught.

Emma . . .

Amy . . .

Emma . . .

Amy Emma?

Emma Yes.

Amy Have you ever been in love? Really.

Emma Of course, I've been in love. I'm in love now. I wouldn't be married to Gary and having a baby if I wasn't in love, would I?

31

Amy I'm only asking, Em, I'm not accusing.

Emma . . .

Amy . . .

Emma What are you not accusing me of?

Amy Sorry?

Emma You said you weren't accusing me.

Amy I'm not.

Emma But you didn't say what you weren't accusing me of?

Amy I'm not not accusing you of anything.
I'm just asking if you've ever been in love.

Emma Really?
. . .
Because it sounds like you're accusing me of gold-digging.

Amy I'm really not.

Emma Good.

A moment.

Amy He is rich, though.

Emma Fuck you.

Amy I mean he has his own plane.

Emma Fuck you.
Also, it's just a Cessna. It's not like it's a jet or anything.

Amy It's a plane.

Emma Look, the fact that that Gary can support me while the baby's small, the fact I can pursue my creativity, the fact I don't have to do sixteen-hour days and case law just to pay the rent . . . yes . . . that is a happy situation which I do appreciate.
But it's not why I'm with him.

Amy You brought it up.

Emma You thought it.

Amy I certainly think it's interesting how quickly you jumped to that assumption.

Emma I adore him.
  I wake up beside him and I smile.
  I cuddle into him on the sofa.
  I watch him at parties.
  He's so light with people, smart and easy, in a good suit.
  I feel proud of him.
  I want him to take care of me.
  I want to mother him.
  Is that love?

Amy I don't know.

Emma I think it is.
  Really.

Emma It's just all those things you said –
  Cuddle.
  Smile.
  Proud.
  Adore.
  The only time I ever feel them.
  Is in the moments after I come.
  And then it's lovely.
  But after a sleep.
  I wake up.
  And it's gone.

Emma It's love.

Amy It's chemicals.

Emma It's love and you should open yourself to it.

Amy How?

Emma You throw up this front, Amy.
Cigarettes and whisky and pants in your handbag.
Because it's cool.
But it's not cool.
You're perfectly capable of love but the moment you're with a man you suspect might conjure it in you – you withdraw.
You're not special. You're not broken. You're just scared.

A moment.

Where the hell is that caretaker?

A moment.

Amy Has Gary made you Christian yet?

Emma I've always been interested in the church.

Amy Interested?

Emma I like the atmosphere, the idea of –

Amy Have you been baptised?

Emma No.

Amy If you die unbaptised, you go to hell. That's what Gary told me.

Emma I'm not ready to be baptised yet.

Emma But you could die at any time.

Emma I don't think that's likely.

Amy You could have an underlying heart condition.

Emma I had a full medical before I got pregnant.

Amy You could be run over by a lorry? Or a terrorist? Or a terrorist in a lorry?
You could die in childbirth.

Emma I'm not ready to be baptised because I don't believe in God.

34

Amy But you go to church?

Emma I like the flowers.

A moment.

Amy Gary fancies me.

Emma No, he doesn't.

Amy Whenever I'm around him, he glows.

Emma Don't be ridiculous.

Amy Every time.
    I can see it happen.
    I arrive at your house. He kisses me on the cheek. He
puts his hand in the small of my back and guides me into
the hall. I hang up my coat and he looks at me and I can see
him think: 'God, I fancy her. I fancy my sister-in-law, and
I bet she'd be up for it if I made a move. I mean, she is quite
slutty.' And then he thinks, 'But, you know what? I won't
make a move. I won't make a move because I'm a Christian.
I'm better than that.'
    And that thought makes him happy and he glows.
    It's a sort of 'Mummy didn't I do well' glow.
    Which, of course, makes me flirt with him terribly for the
rest of the evening.
    Which of course he resists.
    And with each moment of resistance his excitement at
how good he's being grows which makes my desire to
corrupt him grow as well.
    Honestly there's been evenings at your house when I've
been terrifically close to offering to go down on him after
the hors d'oeuvres.
    'Amy, I can't, I'm a married man! Go back to your chair.'

Emma Amy –

Amy God, it would give him such a hard-on to say that.

Emma Don't talk about Gary like that.

35

Amy Like what?

Emma He's my husband.

Amy I know.
I'm sorry.

A moment.

Let me stay with you, Em?
Please.

Emma Okay.
But only for the weekend. Then you have to make some other plans.

Emma If I'm going to write this novel I need to concentrate.

Amy The weekend's all I need.
By Sunday Dan will have calmed down. On Monday I'll crawl back to the spare room. By Friday we'll be back to normal.

Emma Normal?

Amy Normal for us.

Gunshot, a bullet pings off something, a metallic ting.

Emma Jesus, what the fuck was that?

Amy I think those kids are shooting at us.

The Kids have set up an impromptu rifle range.

Emma They have a gun!

Amy It's only an air rifle.

Emma Oh my God.

Another shot.

Amy They aren't shooting at us.

Emma Then what are they shooting at?

The Kids shoot again.

Amy The gulls.

Emma Jesus!

Amy They're not doing any harm.

Emma What do you mean?

Amy They keep missing.

Emma They shouldn't be shooting at anything at all.

A moment.

Amy We used to do stuff like that when we were their age.

Emma We never had a gun.

Amy You once locked a boy in a caravan and said you'd set fire to it.

Emma I did not.

Amy You did. You poured water all over the porch and said it was petrol.
I had to tell you to stop because he'd wet himself.

Emma Is that true?

Amy I remember it like it was yesterday.

Emma Why would I do that?

Amy You were defending me.
He called me a bitch.
You didn't know what it meant but you knew it was mean.

Emma I have no memory.

Amy Kids are shits.

. . .

You should see mine.

. . .

Our Gemma rearranged all the stickers on her friend's Rubik's Cube when she was in the loo. Never told her. She just wanted to watch her not be able to do it in front of the whole class.

Emma Still.

A moment.

Guns. It's not right.

A moment.

(*Shouts.*) Hey!

Amy What are you doing?

Emma (*shouts*) Hey!

Amy Leave it.

Emma (*shouts*) Stop it!

Amy Emma.

Emma Stand in front of me.

Amy What?

Emma In case they shoot.

Amy You want me to take the bullet for you?

Emma I'm pregnant.

A moment.

Amy For fuck's sake.

Amy stands in front of her.

Emma (*to the Kids*) Guys! Guys! Come on. Don't shoot at the birds.

The Kids go quiet.

I know it's fun but –
  Seriously –
  Don't be like that.
  Kids who hurt animals turn into psychopaths.
  You don't want to end up being psychopaths, do you?
  Come on.
  Give me the gun.
  Give me the gun.
  Give me the gun.

— *We weren't shooting at gulls, miss.*

— *We were shooting at tin cans.*

  A Kid shows them some tin cans with bullet holes.

— *We're allowed to.*

— *We do it every night.*

— *The caretaker knows.*

— *We point the gun at the sea.*

— *We know how to do it safely.*

— *My dad's a farmer.*

Emma That's all very well.
  But you could hit somebody.
  You don't know where people might happen to be.
  You could have hit me.
  And I'm pregnant.
  You could have killed my baby.
  How would you feel about that?

  The Kids shrug, uncertain.

Amy Don't worry about her.
  She's writing a book.
  Do any of you want a beer?

  She offers some cans of beer.

Emma (*whispering*) What are you doing?!

Amy We're going to be here for a week, Em. The last thing we need is enemies.

Some Kids take cans.

Amy There you go.
Chill.

A moment, the mood relaxes.

— *You don't look pregnant.*

— *You look like a model.*

Emma Thanks.

— *What sort of a book are you writing?*

Emma A novel.
A novella.
Maybe it's a series of interlinked short stories.

— *What's it about?*

Amy It's about a woman who goes on the run with an escaped prisoner during the war. They're lovers but she's got a husband as well.
And get this, the husband is the leader of the men who're chasing them.

— *Does her husband know it's her he's chasing?*

Amy No.
He thinks she's been killed in a car crash.

Emma Amy.

— *Why's the guy a prisoner?*

Amy They think he's a Nazi spy.

— *Is he a Nazi spy?*

Amy He i,s but – get this – he's also a double agent, working for the British.

— *So, he's a goody?*

Amy Yeah, and she doesn't even know.

Emma Amy –

— *Sounds good.*

Emma It's not really that sort of story.

— *What sort of story is it?*

Emma It's not really a story where things happen.
It's more about how people feel.
. . .

Amy Don't worry.
If it's any good they'll make it into a film.

Emma Whose gun is it, anyway?

A moment.

— *Lance.*

Emma Lance?
Which one of you is Lance?
Which one of you is Lance?

Lance enters, he's in his fifties, in a T-shirt and jeans, slim and weathered . . .

Lance I am.

. . . *I mean, you would.*

Who's asking?

Emma Me.

A moment.

I'm renting this caravan.
   Who are you?

Lance I'm the caretaker.

Emma I'm Emma, this is my sister, Amy.

A moment.

Lance Sorry. I meant to get to you before. I'm running a bit behind today.

Emma Do you have the key?

Lance Sure.
   Come in.

Lance takes a key from his belt and uses it to open the caravan.
   He gestures for Emma to enter.

Please –

She's about to pick up her bags.

Let me.

Emma enters the caravan.
   Lance picks up all the bags and follows.
   Then Amy.
   The Kids watch closely and listen.

(*From inside.*) Bedroom one, bedroom two . . . shower . . . toilet . . .

Lance opens the caravan windows.

. . . this is your kitchen area . . . table folds away . . .

Amy comes outside.
   Lights a cigarette.
   She goes over to sit on a swing, or the roundabout . . . whatever seems easiest.
   The Kids make space for her.

There's a heater and spare blankets in the overhead cupboard but you shouldn't need those. Forecast says it's going to be hot.

There's a fan beside the microwave . . .

Well . . .

If there's anything else?

Emma No, thank you.

Lance Right . . . well.

If anything comes up, I'm in Caravan One, by the bins behind the dance hall.

Just knock.

Any time.

Emma Thank you.

Lance comes out, holding some money, Emma's given him a tip.
A moment.

Amy Hey.

Lance Hey.

Emma (*calling from inside*) Amy!

Are you going to help me put this stuff away or what?

Emma comes out.

Amy, can you get the typewriter from the car?

I need to set up a work station.

She retreats into the caravan.

Amy I gotta . . .

Lance I know.

Lance leaves.
As he leaves, he takes back the gun.
Amy and the Kids watch as he goes.
End of Act One.

Act Two

Lance's caravan.
   Saturday, late morning.
   Heat, sun.

Lance steps out of his caravan carrying a yoga mat.
   *Lance's caravan is his home. Potted plants outside, and
it's painted in a personal colourful way. On the scrappy
concrete patio, he has improvised some garden furniture: a
crate for a table, some camping chairs, and an old beach
umbrella.*
   *On the table, a portable Dansette record player; beside it,
a little stack of LPs.*
   Lance unrolls the yoga mat on the concrete.
   He puts chooses an LP and puts it on: Erik Satie's Trois
Gymnopédies.
   He begins with a salutation to the sun.
   The Kids, sit on a low wall, nearby, and watch.
   Amy enters.
   She sits on the wall with the Kids.
   She watches Lance too.
   He doesn't see her.
   A moment.

Kids You're sixteen, on holiday. What are you wearing?

— A hippy dress, burgundy.

— Track pants, blue and white striped.

— Doc Martens, 501s, long-sleeve Soundgarden T-shirt.

— Private school uniform. Tie loose. Top button undone.

— T-shirt, jeans, socks, no shoes.

— Baggy cargo pants and a midriff top – it's a baby singlet that I bought from Target that I ripped the armpits to fit. I want to be GWEN STEFANI!

— Bathers.

— Polo shirt. It was my year of the polo shirt.

— Grey jeans, white shirt, white dirty Reeboks.

Kids Who are you in love with?

— Karen Bristol. The new girl. Liked the name, liked the body . . .

— Kristian Rooke, because I've been in love with him since I was thirteen. He's tall with brown eyes and he's very skinny. He's three years older than me and calls me Princess. His dad is a drug addict.

— There's the girl next door. There's an air of 'angel' in her. I don't even know her name. The forbidden fruit.

— Seona O'Farrell, because she's pretty and I'm obsessed with her. Her name is like a mantra I used to play any sport better.

— Olivia Dawning. The gorgeous, lovely girl at school who didn't seem to realise it.

— Shane. I love him, he's my crush and my boyfriend. I got the hots for him because he's gorgeous but so quiet at first. Thought he was sexy, surfing. He's a joker now.

— My boyfriend, Anthony, is also my crush. But also the lead singer of The Reels, Dave Mason.

— Nick Garland. He's exceptionally beautiful but I can't talk to him and he's going out with an old school friend. I don't know him, but he seems charming, popular, elusive and terribly sexy.

— Andrew Porter, he's the first person I've met who might be like me.

Kids Amy's wearing the same clothes as yesterday, and she's in love with –

Amy Lance?

> *A moment.*
> *Still holding his yoga pose, Lance turns to see Amy.*
> *He stops.*
> *Relaxes.*
> *Lifts the needle off the turntable.*

Lance Hey.

> *A moment.*

Amy Nothing changes round here.

Lance No.

Amy This must be an antique?

> *She indicates the record player.*

Lance It still goes.

> *A moment.*

Amy You look –

Lance Old?

Amy No.

Lance You do.
I'm joking.

Amy It's okay.

Lance You look great.

> *A moment.*

Amy Do you mind if I sit?

She sits.

Lance Can I get you some coffee? Or juice?

Amy I'm okay.
I just had breakfast with Emma.
You remember Em?
My little sister.

Lance She was a lot smaller then.

Amy She booked the place.
Dunno why.
For old times' sake, I suppose.
I just tagged along.
It didn't occur to me you'd still be here.
Twenty years later.

Lance It's a surprise to me too.

A moment.

Amy Do you still DJ?

Lance As long as they let me.

A moment.

What about you?
What are you . . . up to?

Amy What do I do?

Lance Yes.

A moment.

Amy I choose the music for television programmes.

Lance Ah.

Amy 'Andy and Pete must find a bicycle by five o'clock. It's not going to be easy. Meanwhile Gillian is wrestling with a fondue.' Five, four, three, two, one – 'Little Lion Man' – Mumford and Sons . . . 'Now over to Peter for a look at some of the funnier moments from a glorious week of tennis . . .' Five four three two one – 'How Bizarre' . . .

A moment.

'Liam is sad because his brother's dying of cancer . . .' Five four three two one / Coldplay.

Lance Coldplay.
'Fix You'?

Amy Bingo.
Catalogue knowledge and rights clearance.

A moment.

Lance I'm glad you're still in music.

Amy In music?

Lance When we / were –

Amy What I do bears no relation to what we –

Lance Of course –

Amy It's not even close, Lance.

Lance I know.

Amy Sorry.
It's just . . .

A moment.

We used to sit on that wall.

Lance I remember.

Amy So many teenage bums. It must be worn smooth by now.

Lance It catches the sun.

Amy It's actually physically painful to look at them.
The way they sit, open faces, smooth skin, their lightness,

their spindle-legs, wide eyes, slightly delighted and slightly panicked, as if they're conjuring up the world as they go along and can't quite keep hold of it.

When I look at them it hurts.

Do they . . . do they still . . .?

Lance What?

Amy Dance?

Lance They still dance.

Do you?

A moment.

Amy I used to think you were so sophisticated.

Cooking lasagne.

Watching Swedish movies.

Reading poetry.

My older man.

Lance I was twenty.

A moment.

Amy You said we'd run away, Lance.

We were going to be in a band.

Go to London.

Blow up the world.

Lance I know.

Amy I went to the train station every day.

Every fucking day.

Writing you postcards, sending you notes.

Leaves falling off the trees, wearing my big jumper, rain-soaked jeans.

Making up songs.

You never came.

Lance I'm sorry.

A moment.

Amy It's fine.
I'm fine, Lance. I was fine then. I'm fine now.
It's all fine.
Don't flatter yourself.
Look at me.
I'm perfectly fine.
I'm as totally fine as any woman could possibly be.

He offers her a cigarette.

Lance Here.

She takes it.

Amy Thanks.

A moment.

Lance I missed you.

Amy I missed you too.

A moment.

I got such a shock when I saw you yesterday.

Lance Why didn't you say anything?

Amy I didn't know if you'd remember me.

Lance Of course I remember you.

Amy I was shaking.
Didn't you see?

Lance No.
You seemed so –

Amy What?

Lance Composed.

Amy Composed?

Lance You looked like you were . . . in the place you
needed to be.

With whoever you needed to be with.
I didn't think you would want to be associated with me.

Amy Why, wouldn't I want to be associated with you?

Lance – You're way beyond – you're a –
I'm just the caretaker, Amy.
I thought if I said anything you might just.
Laugh.
Or worse.

A moment.

Amy You're not the only man who's ever let me down, Lance.
Just the first.
There's been dozens since.
I'm only here this weekend because my husband kicked me out.

Lance I'm sorry to hear it.

Amy Don't be. It's good for me.

Lance Why?

Amy Disgrace.
It's good for the soul.
You can't get above yourself when you're sleeping in your car in torn jeggings and a promotional band T-shirt you picked up at work.
When there's a fox on the windscreen and it's looking at you with pity.
It's quite Zen, really, disgrace.
I recommend it.

A moment.

You're smiling.
What are you smiling about?

Lance You.

A moment.

Amy Do you remember our first kiss?

Lance A bit.

Amy What do you remember?

Lance We were writing a song together.

Amy What else?

Lance You were singing it.

Amy What was the song?

Lance I don't remember.

Amy It was 'Summer Special'.

She sings, he joins in.

'Hits on the record player, dancing on the beach,
I wanna kiss my baby,
He's always out of reach,
Summer special, summer special, summer special.'

Amy What else do you remember?

A moment.

Lance I remember the knitted top you wore. I remember your hair was so hard with hairspray it cracked when I touched it. I remember you biting my lip when you kissed me. I remember the snake belt on your jeans.

Amy I wasn't wearing jeans.

Lance I remember a snake belt.

Amy I was wearing a skirt.

Lance Are you sure?

Amy My legs were wet from the rain.

Lance Was it raining?

Amy Very lightly.

Lance I didn't notice.

Amy Do you remember where we were?

Lance Behind the last of the caravans?

Amy We were in the dunes.

Lance Of course.

Amy What time was it?

Lance Are you interrogating me?

Amy I'm just curious.

Lance It was late.
I'd finished my set.
The ballroom had closed.
We were high.

A moment.

You were singing.
You walked into my arms, and I held you.
I kissed you.
You kissed me back and then your knees gave.

Amy Gave?

Lance Yes.

Amy I don't remember that.

Lance You dropped, heavy in my hands, buckled and
I lowered you down.

Amy I pulled you down I was so desperate for you.
Your white T-shirt, your hair all over your face like Joey
Ramone.
You did that smile thing –
You still do it.

Lance I remember looking at you, lying beside you on the marram grass, your eyes wide, the stars behind you.
I remember looking at you and thinking you must be the most beautiful girl in the whole county.

Amy The whole county?

Lance For sure.

Amy County?

Lance What's wrong with that?

Amy Nothing.
It's just, as a compliment, it feels rather . . . pinched.

Lance Pinched?

Amy Not the most beautiful girl you'd ever seen?
Not the most beautiful girl in the world?
The most beautiful girl in the county?

Lance That's about half a million people.
It's actually a pretty massive compliment.

Amy My desire for you was like the universe, Lance.
I wanted you in a way that fucking burned.
So, it's a tiny bit insulting that, in that same moment.
You were calibrating me against a county boundary.

A moment.

Lance The county was the limit of my world, Amy.
I'd never been anywhere else.

A moment.
A moment.
A moment.

Amy You told me you'd DJ'd in Ibiza.

Lance Did I?

Amy You definitely did.

Lance Okay. So, I'd been to Ibiza once.

Amy You said you did it every winter.

Lance I went a few times. But it was basically just a flight there and back.
The county is what I know.

Amy You're such a fucking player, Lance.
Fucked by a fucking provincial player.
A provincial . . . fucking . . .
Such a cliché.
I wanted to be a rock star.
I thought I was special.
My entire fucking life's a fucking cliché.

A moment.
  A moment.
  A moment.

Lance Amy.
Right now.
With the sun on the water.
Looking at you.
You are are . . .
Without question.
The most beautiful woman in the whole municipal district.

Amy And I bet you know them all.

A moment.
  It's okay.

Lance If we were on a television programme and you were underscoring this moment.
What would you play?
Come on.

Amy is intrigued, she thinks, she looks at her phone . . .

'Meanwhile Lance and Amy catch up on old times.'
Five four three two one –

Amy presses play –
  Spike Jones's 'My Old Flame'.
  At first it's quite apposite, almost moving.
  And then it breaks into a comical cacophony of sirens,
trumpet and swannee whistle.
  They both laugh.
  Emma enters.
  Amy switches off the music.

Amy Emma?

Emma What are you doing here?

Amy Nothing.
  I'm just hanging out.

Emma With the caretaker?

Amy It's allowed, isn't it.

Emma Of course . . . only you said you were going into
town to buy painkillers.
  After the amount you drank.
  Last night.

Amy I did.
  And then on the way back I bumped into Lance.

Emma Bumped into.

Amy You remember Lance?

Emma From yesterday.

Amy Do you remember when we used to come here with
Mum and Dad?
  When we were kids –
  Lance was the DJ.

Emma Is that true?

Lance Guilty as charged.

Emma I don't remember.

Amy You were too young.
We were just catching up.

A moment.

Lance Is there something I can help you with?

Emma There's a problem with the fridge.

Lance What sort of problem?

Emma A buzz.
A sort of a low vibratory buzz.

Lance That can happen.

Emma Can it?

Lance There's a small motor mechanism that powers the refrigerator unit. Sometimes if the ice in the freezer gets to a very particular weight it can get caught into a vibration cycle with some of the other components and it ends up making a noise.

Emma I wouldn't mind but I'm trying to write.

Lance It should fix itself eventually.

Emma It's distracting.

Lance You could put some headphones on?

Amy There's always something distracting when you're trying to write.

Lance It usually goes away after about five minutes.

Amy Or you could take a break?

Emma I'm in mid-flow.

Lance Give it five minutes, then we'll go and have a look.

A moment.

Emma I suppose I could do with a break.

Lance Would you like coffee?

Emma Sure.

> *Emma sits.*
> *He gives her coffee from the cafetière.*
> *A moment.*

Lance What are you writing?

Emma A novel.

Amy It's more of a novella. Possibly a series of interlinked short stories.

Lance How's it going?

Emma It was going great.
    Until the fridge.
    I put the little camping table up at the window.
    Set up the typewriter.
    Got my notebook and pen.
    There's no internet here so that's a bonus.
    Looked out at the sea and.
    I just thought . . . how would I tell this story if I was telling it to one of my girlfriends, you know, over brunch or something . . .
    And the words just came pouring out.

Amy In the right order?

Lance What sort of words?

Emma Just words about a typical day in the life of a French woman in a small town in 1939, how she buys bread and cycles through the vineyard, and argues with the farmer, and then in the afternoon she has to do all this admin work for the Resistance.
    Her husband's the mayor.

He works in the 'Mairie'.
When the town bell rings, she thinks about him.

Lance It sounds good.

Emma I just think, if you're enjoying the writing . . . that's all you can do.

Lance It must have been annoying about the fridge then.

Emma Really annoying.

Lance Should fix itself shortly.

Amy All that good stuff.

Emma I just need to trust . . . I suppose . . .

Amy This too shall pass.

A moment.
Emma takes out a notebook and writes something down.
A moment.

Did you just write down 'This too shall pass'?

Emma Yes.
So?

Amy You know that's from the Bible?

Emma I just thought it sounded nice.

Amy It's a fundamental summation of the healing power of transience.
But, yeah.
Nice.

Lance It's Rumi.

Amy What?

Lance 'This too shall pass.' It's not the Bible. It's Rumi.
An Iranian medieval poet.

Amy I know who Rumi is?

Emma I've got a Rumi poster in my office.
'Somewhere in the middle of right and wrong there is a field. I will meet you there.'

Amy Bit edgy for a lawyer's office.

Emma That is Rumi, isn't it?

Lance I'm not sure about the translation but it's very much in line with Sufi philosophy so probably.

Emma It's nice.

A moment.
Emma takes out her notebook and writes something down.
A moment.

Why don't they go somewhere else?

Lance They like it here.

Emma There's a whole clifftop walk, there's benches, views across the bay.
There's birds.
Why don't they do something?

Lance They like the wall.

Emma I remember sitting there.
Day after day.
Music from Amy's cassette player.
Dancing.
. . . what was that song . . .

She sings half-remembered lines from 'Haven't Stopped Dancing Yet' by Gonzales.
Amy joins in . . . They remember more.
A moment of joy.

Do you still play that one?

Lance Sometimes.

A moment.

Emma Tell me about Holiday Heaven.

Lance What about it?

Emma Why's it for sale?

Lance Sign of the times, I guess.

Emma What do you mean?

Lance It was built in the sixties by a local guy. He'd been to France. When he was there he saw a campsite with tennis courts and pétanque, and a communal dining hall. He thought he'd bring the dream here. So, he bought the land off a farmer, put a few units on the slope to the beach, and called it Holiday Heaven. It grew and grew all through the seventies. Then he put in the amusement arcade, rifle range, the ballroom.

Emma I remember the penny falls.

Lance I just hung about.
   One day he put up an advert for a DJ.
   He auditioned me . . . Empty hall, box of records, low winter sun coming in the big window.
   He sat in the middle of the dance floor on a bucket chair smoking Gauloises.
   I was just out of school.
   I didn't know what he wanted so I said 'This is "Stayin' Alive" by the Bee Gees, going out to Joan and Kev in Caravan Seven.' He gave me the job on the spot.
   Standards were never high.
   In the eighties he sold the place to a timeshare company. In the nineties the timeshare company were bought by a hotel group who were bought by an airline.
   About five years later a venture capital company bought the airline and broke it up into pieces which they sold on

separately and in that deal we ended up with a ski resort in Bulgaria owned by an Italian pension fund.

Couple of months ago they wrote to us and said the fund had gone bust in the credit crunch and they had to sell their assets.

Probably took them a year or two to even realise they owned the place.

I doubt it's ever made them any money.

Couple of months ago a guy came round to take pictures.

Amy Is there a buyer?

Lance Not yet.

People go on holiday abroad, now? They go to Gambia or Bali or the Maldives. Who'd buy a place like this?

Maybe they'll build houses.

Amy What will you do?

Lance I don't know.

I can live in a caravan.

I'll be all right.

A moment.
Emma takes out her notebook and writes something down.
A moment.

Emma Do you think we could go and look at the fridge now?

Lance Sure.

Lance picks up his tool bag.
Emma and Lance leave.
A moment.
One Kid plays with music on her phone.
Amy watches her.
Amy joins the Kids on the wall.

Amy When I was your age, I had a beatbox. It was really big and clunky. I carried it about by the handle. I used to

play the same song over and over again . . . I'd walk up and down that wall for a whole afternoon.
 Used to drive Lance mad.

— *Is Lance your boyfriend?*

Amy No.

— *Was he your boyfriend back then?*

Amy Not really.

— *But you loved him?*

Amy I thought it was love.

— *Do you want to get back together with him?*

Amy No!
 – We're just . . .
 It's nice to see an old friend.

— *What was the song you used to listen to?*

Amy It doesn't matter, it's old. It's boring.
 I want to know about your music.
 Tell me about your music.
 What do you like?

— *Anything.*

— *Everything.*

Amy What's your absolute favourite song. Right now. If you had to pick one song.

One Kid tells her the name of a song.

Why do you like that one?

They tell her why they like the song.

Is it on your phone?

The Kids play the song.
 They all listen for a bit.

Can you write it into my phone.

She gives her phone to a Kid, who types in the name of the band for her.

— *You've got a text.*

Amy Give it here.

The Kids don't give it.

— *It's your 'Beloved Husband'.*

Amy Don't read my texts!

— *He says he's worried about you.*

Amy He shouldn't be.

— *'Where are you? Are you all right? You've been away for five days. I feel afraid for your safety.'*

— *You've been away for five days?*

Amy It's complicated.

— *But he doesn't know where you are.*

Amy He's being dramatic.

— *'You need to look after yourself.'*

Amy . . .

— *'Your kids need you.'*

Amy This how he speaks to psychotic people he finds on the street.
He's trained to speak like this.
He thinks I'm drunk.

— *'Would you be willing to reply to this text to let me know you're safe.'*

Amy Give it here.

She goes to take the phone back from them, but they keep it.

— *It's not right to leave your husband worried.*

Amy He'll cope.

— *What does he do?*

Amy Do?

— *What's his job?*

Amy He's a paramedic.

— *He sounds nice.*

Amy He is nice. He's bloody perfect. That's his problem.
He's kind.
Modest.
Does puppet shows. Makes vegan baby food. Volunteers at the school.
He'd be so much easier to live with if he had a cocaine habit.
Don't take cocaine.
That's not me telling you to take cocaine.

— *He's feeling sad.*

Amy Yeah well.

— *He loves you.*

Amy Everybody loves somebody.

— *Is he at home looking after your kids right now?*

Amy Yeah.

The Kids think that's a bit dodgy.

Amy He's better with the kids than me.

— *You should call him.*

— *You should go back to him.*

65

— You should at least text him.

— Here.

— We wrote a text.

— We're going to send it.

Amy No. Hey.

Kids send text.
The Kids give her back her phone.

'I'm okay. Need space. Broken-heart emoji.'
What's your name, kid?

Kid says their name.

Fuck you, [*Kid's name*].

Emma has re-entered.
She sits on the wall, next to Amy.

Emma What did they send?

Amy shows her.

Amy Where's Lance?

Emma He's chipping ice off the freezer.

A moment.

Amy You knew who he was, yesterday, didn't you?
When he came over with the keys.

Emma Of course.

A moment.

Amy You should go back to your writing?

Emma I'm not feeling inspired.

Amy I thought you said the words were pouring out?

Emma It was mostly notes.
Notes are pouring out.
I'll write the actual words later.

Amy I was thinking about the novel.
I think you're missing a trick.
The German should be the mayor of a small country town in Bavaria.
So that when Jacques interrogates him, he should find that out.
And that's something they have in common.
And so they develop a grudging respect for each other.

A moment.

Aren't you going to note that down?

Emma It's not really that sort of book.

A moment.

Amy It's nearly lunchtime.

Emma What will we do now?

Amy I don't know.

— *There's a party later.*

— *In the ballroom.*

Emma What sort of party?

— *Last night of the holidays.*

— *Everybody gets dressed up.*

— *Old people come too.*

— *Anybody can come as long as you dress up.*

Emma What do you think?

Amy I don't know, Emma, it's not really my scene.

Emma Come on.
  You need to cheer up.

Amy I've nothing to wear.

— *You look great.*

— *You look cool.*

— *You just need something tight.*

— *I've got a dress you can borrow.*

Amy All right. All right. Jesus.

> *The Kids cheer.*
> *The Kids' song plays.*
> *Day turns to afternoon.*
> *Afternoon turns to night.*
> *Emma and Amy transform . . .*
> *End of Act Two.*

Act Three

The ballroom balcony.
Saturday night.
Heat, darkness.

The great glass windows of the ballroom look out over the sea.
Inside, dancing is in full swing.
When the doors to the ballroom are closed, the sound is muted, but when the doors open, music thunders out.
On the balcony there are picnic tables, chairs and umbrellas.
The Kids lounge around in their party gear, resting from the dancing.

Kids You're sixteen, you're on holiday, what's your favourite song?

— 'Mambo No. 5'.

— 'Even Flow' – Pearl Jam.

— 'Jive Talkin'' – The Bee Gees.

— Savage Garden?!

— 'Throw Your Arms Around Me' – Hunters and Collectors.

— 'My Humps' – Black Eyed Peas.

— 'Vienna' by Ultravox, I think.

— 'Benny and the Jets'.

— Dance music, house music. I love S-Express.

Kids How do you dance?

— All crazy and free arms, a bit side to side.

— Funky.

— Headbang, mosh or nothing.

— Self-consciously.

— Really well and I know it.

— Wildly.

— Stupidly.

— I don't. Not yet.

— I was a dancer at that age, about to go into the profession. So, I'm really good.

> *The doors to the ballroom fly open. Music pours out and, with it . . .*
> *Emma and Amy, giggling and sweating.*
> *Amy swigs from a bottle of wine, Emma lights a cigarette.*
> *They settle down at a picnic table.*

Emma Listen.
I've been thinking.
And I've had an idea.

Amy About what?

Emma About Holiday Heaven.

Amy What about it?
Dunnimore should buy it.

Amy What's Dunnimore?

Emma Dunnimore's my company.

Amy I didn't know you had a company.

Emma Mine and Gary's company. It was Gary's company originally but I'm a partner now.

Amy What does it do?

Emma It's a vehicle.

Amy A vehicle for what?

Emma Opportunity.
We identify value in failing assets and then recover that value for our shareholders.

Amy Okay so . . .

Emma A company might be for sale. Maybe they make mattresses. They can't make a profit any more because of cheap mattresses being made in China. So, the company's being sold off cheap. But there might still be value. Maybe the workforce is skilled. So Dunnimore buys the company. We halve the workforce, sell the land around the factory, then launch a new brand that makes bespoke artisanal seating for traditional pubs.
Every transaction makes a profit.
We recover the value.

Amy I always wondered what you really did.

Emma What I really did?

Amy Your job.

Emma I'm a lawyer.

Amy I know you're a lawyer but, I mean – it's not as if I've ever seen you in court.

Emma That's not the sort of law I practise.

Amy To be honest, I never really thought about it.

Emma Clearly.

Amy It's not as if you ever got a man off death row in Mississippi or anything.

Emma Amy, I'm a corporate lawyer.

Amy All right, no reason to be sensitive, I'm not judging.

Emma I'm not being sensitive, and you are judging.

Amy I'm not.
I just never realised what you did, that's all.
So, it's interesting.

A moment.

You work for a company –

Emma I own a company.

Amy And that company could buy Holiday Heaven.

Emma Exactly.

Amy Where's the value in an old holiday camp?

Emma Childhood.

Amy Childhood.
Look at it. The ballroom, the penny falls, the seawater pool . . . It's so familiar, so warm, so innocent. This place is our childhood but now we can live in it.

Amy Do people want to live in their childhood?

Emma Of course!

Amy Some of us didn't want to at the time.

Emma Okay, maybe not live.
But take a holiday.
And it isn't childhood, exactly. It's childhood with a warm glow.
We repaint the chalets, install Wi-Fi, modernise the menu, put on craft beers, provide a crèche and a kids' club; market the place at young families.

Amy It sounds like a lot of work.

Emma It's my post-pregnancy project.

Amy I thought the baby was your post-pregnancy project?

Emma It is.

They both are.

Sitting at the camping table this morning, staring out the window at the sea, I just realised for the first time in years, for the first time ever in my life maybe.

I felt content.

I think it was the simplicity.

One room, one fridge, one task.

Simple.

Even the sea's simple . . . like a painting by Rothko.

Amy Have you been smoking Lance's weed?

Emma I mean it, Amy.

Dunnimore will buy Holiday Heaven and I'll supervise the renovation.

I'll appoint an experienced manager, for the day-to-day tasks.

I'll live on site, with the little one, in Paradise.

Amy I don't want to piss on your parade –

Emma Then don't.

Amy Em, a baby takes a lot of energy.

Emma I know that.

Jesus, Amy! I'm not an idiot.

I'll have a nanny.

Amy Right.

Emma Probably two, to be honest.

They'll live in the next-door caravan.

A moment.

Amy Where's Gary in this picture?

Emma Gary's busy, Amy. Gary works eighteen-hour days.

We'd still have the house in the city.

That's the beauty of it.
The city's only thirty minutes away.
This place could be our haven.
A refuge.
The three of us together.
Cuddled in a heap.

Amy Just you, Gary, the baby, and the two nannies.

Emma So much love.

Amy It's a nice dream.

Emma There's no such thing as dreams, Amy.
There's only things you do do, and things you don't.

A moment.

Amy What about Lance?

Emma What about him?

Amy Is he childhood, or will he have to go in the clear-out?

Emma I don't know.
He was pretty good with the fridge.
He's skilled –

Amy Like the mattress people.

Emma Exactly.
And I think he has a good seventies image.

Amy One for the mums.

Emma What?

Amy Come on, I saw you looking at him.

Emma Amy, don't.

Amy You fancy him. It's obvious.

Emma Don't do this.

Amy Do what?

Emma Not everyone's like you, you know.

Amy So?

Emma You want me to validate your damage by participating in it.

Amy Damage?

Emma A life spent in pursuit of unreachable men?

Amy Reaching them, thank you very much, rather more often than not.

Emma Sleeping with them, maybe.

Amy What's wrong with that.

Emma So, you don't think you're damaged?
Is that what you're saying?

Amy No, of course not.
Of course I'm damaged.
I'm forty-three. Who isn't?
But that doesn't mean I've been damaged by men.

Emma By who then?

Amy I don't know, by the world.
Capitalism.
Patriarchy.

Emma Grow up, Amy.

Amy Grow up?
Like you?
Grow up like a nice normal lady, with a nice normal husband, in a nice normal suburb and fall into that nice normal thing you call love, and never be surprised again, never explore, never expand, never break the boundaries of anyone, ever again, even though, as I'm sure you'll agree – we only get put on this earth once.
And as you so wisely put it –

There's no such thing as dreams.
There's only things you do do, and things you don't.
Well, my life is a great big, damaged heap, Em.
But it's a great big, damaged heap of things I've done.
And yours is just a great big heap of things you didn't.

A moment.

Emma Every time you talk about love you preface it.

Amy I what?

Emma You say 'so-called' love, or 'nice normal' love.
It's almost like you're afraid of it.

Amy Why would I be afraid of love?

Emma Because it might heal you.

Amy How do you know it wasn't love that damaged me?

Emma Because you've never experienced it.

Amy What makes you think I've never experienced love?

Emma Have you?

A moment.

You'll be all right.
   You just need to get over yourself. It's not your job to
carry off the sins of the world. You're not Christ the
Redeemer, you're a middle-aged mum with an ache in the
fanjo. Get over it. Look after your kids. Work. Smile. Go on
picnics. Watch TV.
   It's not difficult.

Amy It is for me.

Emma It's just work.

Amy Hard labour.

Emma Why do you always have to be so fucking dark?

Amy No, no, you're right. That's my choice. A life sentence of hard labour. Or –

Emma Or you can stay permanently sad.

A moment.

Come on, I'm ready to dance again.

She drinks some more wine.

Amy I thought you weren't drinking.

Emma I'm breaking boundaries.
I thought you'd approve.
Come on!

Another drink.

Amy You go.
I'll come in a bit.

Emma leaves, the doors swing open, sound, the doors swing closed.
Amy is left with the Kids.
She approaches them.

Any of you got a fag?

— *No.*

— *No. Sorry.*

— *Not me.*

— *I don't smoke.*

Amy No. Of course you don't. Very good.
No booze, no fags.
You'll dye your hair blue, you'll have threesomes, you'll do ketamine and consider polyamory, you'll put a stud in your eye and a bone in your nose but you won't smoke.

— *That's quite a clichéd view of young people.*

Amy I'm sorry.

— *Teenagers are not a homogenous group.*

Amy No.

— *We're individuals.*

Amy I was an individual once, myself.

— *You still are.*

Amy Sadly, I think I'm just the latest, well-thumbed edition of a very old story.

A moment.

Have really none of you got a fag?

One Kid stands forward.
This Kid's the one in the group who's quiet but who's also cool.
Thoughtful.
A boy, or a tomboy.

You're a life-saver.

Amy and the Kid sit together, drink and smoke.

Amy How old are you?

— *Seventeen.*

Amy Do you work out?

The Kid answers.

We didn't have gyms when I was your age. We prized weakness. I don't know why. Everyone looked like they were on heroin.

The Kid answers.

I wish I was your age.
    The thing about being young is, there's so much fucking choice. I mean literally everybody is potentially available

and they're all hot. Or at least . . . there's an infinite amount of hot. If there isn't someone hot for you in your town, there'll be more in the next, or the next, or the next. There is what you would describe as a 'plenitude' of sexual opportunity. It's like standing in the orange juice section of an American supermarket. There's just so much fucking orange juice. It's astonishing. So . . . what you find is . . . instead of focusing on sex, you focus on love. You do the equivalent of saying to yourself, amongst all of these cartons of orange juice, which one truly cares for me? Kia-Ora – it's the perfect orange juice. Kia-Ora gets me. And you buy it because, if Kia-Ora loves you, that means you are not making a mistake by ignoring all the other orange juices on the shelf. If you and Kia Ora have a special bond, you needn't expend any of your emotion worrying about the infinite abyss of possibility waiting to suck you into its existential void.

You drink Kia-Ora.

And you are happy.

Then, as you get older, slowly, the orange juice starts disappearing from the shelves. There's fewer and fewer brands . . . and you're, like, still drinking the Kia-Ora but, you know, being honest, you're a bit sick of the taste of it and . . . are you going to die without having ever even fucking tasted Del Monte . . . ? Do you see? As choice declines the need becomes physical. Is it orange. Is it juice. Is it on the shelf? Great. Fuck it. Life's too short.

A sudden thunder of music as the great doors to the ballroom open.

Lance comes out; he's carrying beers.

Some other Kids come out with him.

Some excitement and rearranging of the places around the table.

Lance sits in the middle.

He takes out a little joint, and lights it.

Lance I love this time of year.

Amy Shouldn't you be on the decks?

Lance Playlist.

Amy It's good.

Lance I saw you dancing.

He offers her his spliff.
She takes it.
A moment.

Amy Look at you?

Lance What?

Amy Sitting there as if nothing in the world has ever troubled you, as if nothing in the world could ever trouble you. You're permanent, Lance, like a – like a – rock formation, a peculiar rock formation that, from a distance, you might think is a giant man looking out over the sea, but when you get up close you see it's just rocks, set down long ago, by a glacier or something and yes, one of them might be balanced on top of another, yes it might look dramatic, but the truth is, it's never going to fall, not in our lifetime, not while there's humans here to see it.
It's no wonder people worship you.

Lance Nobody worships me, Amy.
I'm just living my life.

Amy Tide goes in.
Tide goes out.
Stars spiral around the horizon.
And every summer some woman comes along.
And sees you sitting there smoking on the deck.
And mistakes you for the still point in the turning of the universe.
She thinks you might be her only tilt at eternity.
Her chance at something great or grand.
And she lets drop every defence she has.

All her cynicism, all her intellect, all her irony.
She willingly climbs out from behind her castle walls.
And offers herself to you.

. . .

And all the while.
Lance.
You were not still, you were not Zen, you were not wise.
You were not eternal.
You were stagnant.
You were stuck.
All that was great or grand in you, gone.
Long ago.

Lance Amy.

Amy Yes.

Lance I feel like we're inevitably going to fuck.
I'm just wondering if we should do it now.
Or later.

Amy We could not do it.

Lance We both know that's not going to happen.

Amy Why not?

Lance Because we're alive.
Because we're here.

A moment.

Amy The song's coming to an end.

Lance I know.

Amy Can I have go on the decks?

Lance You want to DJ?

Amy Just for a bit.

A moment.

Lance Sure.

Amy Is the set-up the same as it used to be?

Lance Pretty much.

> *Amy swigs some whisky.*
> *Amy kisses him.*
> *Amy opens the doors.*
> *Music thunders out.*
> *Emma comes out, just as Amy goes in.*

Emma (*shouting*) Where you going?

Amy (*shouting*) To lose myself.

> *The doors swing shut.*
> *The music is muted again.*
> *A moment.*
> *Emma sits down not far from Lance.*
> *Lance continues to smoke his joint.*
> *Emma watches.*
> *The last song finally ends and there is a moment of sickening quiet . . .*
> *Lance stiffens . . . Will he have to save the day?*
> *The moment stretches.*
> *Until . . . suddenly . . .*
> *'Sugar Baby Love' by The Rubettes comes thundering out of the speakers.*
> *All the teenagers listen.*
> *One teenager holds the great doors to the ballroom open.*
> *Lance and Emma listen.*
> *Lance smiles.*
> *Emma closes her eyes.*
> *Some of the teenagers dance . . .*
> *Some time before the song ends, the teenager lets the doors swing shut.*
> *Once more the music is muted.*

Emma That oldie, so corny.

Lance The kids like it.

Emma It's hardly sexy.

Lance Kids don't like songs about sex.
They like songs about love.

Emma Is that right?

Lance That's my experience.

A moment.

Emma Do you have a lot of experience?

Lance Some.

A moment.

Emma Do you think you could manage this place?

Lance Which place.

Emma Holiday Heaven.

Lance Manage it?

Emma That's what I'm asking.

Lance Elizabeth is the manager.

Emma For now.

Lance What do you mean?

Emma Do you think you could be the manager.

Lance It's not something I've ever really thought about.

Emma Come on.
You know this place better than anyone.
You know how it works.
You know what people want.

Lance Do I?

Emma I've seen how you control the floor.

Lance Control the floor?

Emma With your decks.

Lance Oh . . . yeah . . . but that's . . . I mean . . .
Management.
There's a lot of.
Invoices.

Emma That's actually a common misconception.
Management isn't about invoices.

Lance Isn't it?

Emma It's about choices.
Feeling a situation.
Judging possibilities.
Simultaneously seeing five steps ahead.
And being wholly and completely in the present.
It's a lot like being a DJ.

A moment.

I'll be straight with you.
I'm interested in buying Holiday Heaven.
Run it as an independent enterprise.
Repackage the package, emphasise simplicity, improve
the menus.
A carefully curated retro-modernist aesthetic.
I think there's an opportunity here.
But I've seen what you can do with a crowd.
I'm only interested if this place comes with you attached.
How would you like to be the boss?

Lance I don't know, it sounds like a lot of admin.

Emma Admin's just a line in the budget, Lance.
I'd sign you up for a five-year contract.
A hundred K a year.
Car.

Accomodation.
Pension.
So, what do you say?

A moment.

Lance Wow.

A moment.

Emma I know, right?
It's genius, isn't it.
You know how sometimes you just know something is right.
You just know that the universe is offering you something.
And it's up to you to take it.
Some people see those things, some people don't.
You do, I do.
The fruit is there for the taking.
Take it.

A moment.
   The big doors swing open.
   Teenagers leave the dance floor.
   Music thunders out behind them.
   Something old and punk.
   The doors swing shut.
   The music is muted.

Lance Oh Jesus.

Emma What?

Lance She'll empty the dance floor.

Lance gets up to go inside.

Emma Wait.

Lance What?

Emma Do you do requests?

Lance No.

Lance leaves.
As he opens the big ballroom doors, the music thunders out.
As the doors swing shut behind him, the music is muted.
Emma is alone, slightly giddy, glowing.
A Kid approaches her.
They're confident, older-seeming than the others, bright.
Pretty.

— *Hey.*

Emma Hey.

— *What's your name?*

Emma I'm Emma.

— *I think you look really amazing, Emma.*

Emma . . .

— *I mean it. You look really amazing. So beautiful. Not beautiful like off of TV – I mean – you're like a movie star who's in indie movies – like Greta Gerwig – I don't mean you look like Greta Gerwig because you don't. I just mean that you look – amazing.*

Emma You're very sweet.

— *I mean it.*
Will you kiss me?

Emma What?

The other Kids, who have been watching this, laugh.
It's clear there are an audience here and they are in on this.

— *Would you kiss me?*

Emma You want me to kiss you?

— *Yeah.*

Emma I don't think that would be appropriate.

— *Why not?*

Emma Because you are considerably younger than me.

— *I'm eighteen.*

Emma Still.

— *Don't you like me?*

Emma No, it's not that.

— *What then?*

Emma I'm married.

— *Just a kiss.*

> *A moment.*
> *The Kid whispers in Emma's ear.*
> *We can't hear.*
> *A moment.*

Emma Take your chewing gum out of your mouth.

> *Kid takes chewing gum out of mouth.*
> *Emma kisses Kid.*
> *Quite a good kiss.*
> *The Kids squeal, cheer and are delighted.*
> *She stops.*
> *A moment.*
> *The Kid staggers away, dazed.*
> *The doors open and . . .*
> *Lance's voice thunders out over the PA.*

Lance (*over the PA*) Ladies and gentlemen, we're coming
right to the end of the evening, it's been a wonderful end to
a wonderful holiday week here at Holiday Heaven, we've

had a lot of fun, we've made a lot of friends, and we hope we'll see you all next year. So come on now, it's time for you all to pick you partners for the last dance. Don't be shy now. Fortune favours the brave. The last song's always a very special one, and this time, it's going out to someone very special . . . someone staying in Paradise . . .

> *Lance plays a gorgeous old slow song.*
> *Emma goes inside.*
> *The Kids all choose partners, out on the balcony.*
> *Amy comes out, whisky glass in hand.*
> *Amy has been drinking hard.*
> *She sways.*
> *She sees the Kids, dancing in pairs.*
> *She sees Emma watching the Kids dance.*
> *For a moment the scene is beautiful . . . elegiac . . .*
> *even optimistic.*
> *Amy takes out her phone.*

Amy Woman dancing. Happy face. Dolphin leaping. Fairy. Heart. Whale. Heart. Kiss. Kiss. Kiss.

> *Amy sways.*
> *Amy drinks.*

Send.

> *End of Act Three.*

Act Four

Inside Lance's Caravan.
Sunday, early hours.
Heat, darkness.

Lance enters the caravan, followed by Emma and a swaying
Amy.
    They stumble and laugh.
    Lance switches on the lights.
    It's too bright, Amy and Emma react with horror.
    In the sudden brightness we see the living room of
Lance's caravan, dominated by over two decades' worth of
accumulated stuff: movie posters, second-hand books,
DVDs and various items of pop-cultural memorabilia
and . . .
    Arranged around the caravan interior: the Kids.
    The caravan is small, so to fit them all in takes
imagination. They sit on countertops, tucked into corners,
cross-legged on the floor, lying on top of the sofa like cats.
    It's not entirely clear if they are 'there' in any real sense,
or if they are ghosts.
    In any case, the Kids watch the trio as they drunkenly
arrive and settle into the caravan's cramped social space.
    Lance uses a dimmer switch to bring the lights down low.
    He switches on some mood lighting.

Emma Jesus –

Lance Sorry about the – mess –

Amy – That smell –

Lance – I can open a window –

Amy – No, it's – nice.

Emma – Cosy –

Lance – I didn't expect visitors –

Amy – I remember it –

Lance – I can spray something –

Amy – It's heady –

Emma – You need to sit down –

Amy – The smell of books and records and dope and man.

Lance – Would anyone like a drink –

Emma – Have you got herbal tea –

> *Lance puts the kettle on.*
> *Amy and Emma sit, polite guests on the banquette.*

Is this caravan a 'Nirvana', Lance?

Lance What? Oh, I don't know.

Emma May I look around.

Lance Sure.

> *Emma goes to look around.*

Amy She's thinking of buying.

Lance She told me.

Amy Did she?

Lance She did.

Amy She's got big ideas.
Big plans.

> *Amy gets up.*
> *She picks up the air rifle.*
> *She aims it at Lance.*

Lance I'd feel more relaxed if you put the gun down.

She puts it down.
He picks it up and puts it on a stand.

Emma (*from off*) Does the shower come as standard?

Lance I think so.

A moment.

Amy This place hasn't changed.

Lance More books.

A moment.

Emma (*from off*) Fucking hell, Lance!

Lance What?

Emma (*from off*) You have so many records!

Emma enters.

He has a room full of records.

Amy I know.

Emma You should see it.
The second bedroom – it's just full – wall to wall.
No room for anything else.
I'm surprised the floor can bear the weight of it.

Lance It's my job, I guess.

Emma And they're all in alphabetical order.

Lance They're not all alphabetical.
Some of it's – by category.

Amy – By category.
Floor-fillers, smoochers, one for the grans, one for the kids.

Lance You remember?

Amy Of course I do.

Amy pours herself a Jack Daniel's from Lance's bottle.

Emma Instead of that room. You could just have Spotify.

Lance I know.

Emma A hard drive.
  The size of a paperback.
  Or even store them in the cloud.

Lance I like to hold them.

Amy Records were always things my boyfriends had. If I liked a song, I remembered it. I could remember whole libraries of music. Sometimes, in a pub quiz, there'd be some man or other going on about how music was his specialist subject, and how you could ask him any question and he'd know, and I would be quiet, and he'd think I was just a girl but then –
  Bam bam bam.
  Even at eighteen.
  I could wipe the floor with them.

Emma Now we have phones.

Amy It's not the same.

Amy opens up the Dansette.

Can I play something?

Lance Sure.

Emma Make it something good.

Amy exits to look at records.
Lance hands Emma a mug of tea.
A moment.

You look good.

Lance Do I?

Emma Fit.
  What's your regime?

Lance I don't really . . .
Yoga.

Emma You could do yoga on that balcony. On a summer morning you could just pour yourself out of bed in your pyjamas, grab a coffee, put some music on and just . . . stretch . . . just stretch out your body in the sun.

Lance It gets pretty breezy out there.

Emma I like the wind. I like to feel nature on my skin. The city's awful. You can smell the petrol fumes coming up from the street. People shouting and fighting all night. Don't get me wrong. I like drama, but in the end, as you get older, something changes, doesn't it?

Lance I guess so.

Emma I'm tired of the gym, I'm tired of control – I want sky, the ocean, wildness.
Do you know what I mean?

Lance I know what you mean.

A moment.
Amy comes back in carrying an album.

Amy (*to Emma*) You're still here.

Emma Where else would I be.

Amy I thought you might have – I don't know, fucked off, or something.

Emma I'm enjoying myself.

Amy Don't you have a book to write?

Emma When you're being creative you have to cut loose sometimes.

A moment.

Amy When I last put a record on this machine.

You were asleep on the bed.

The sun was lying across your body.

And the record was *16 Lovers Lane* by The Go-Betweens.

I remember you'd bought it in town the day before.

I remember holding the square of the sleeve in my hand like this.

Carefully taking the record out, sliding my hand in, finger in the hole, so as not to smudge the vinyl, just like you taught me.

Looking at the shine.

Excited.

Because everything was new then, everything single thing was new.

My monkey boots, my black tights, my Breton top.

My Gauloises Blondes cigarettes.

And music.

I was a song being made.

You can only hear a song for the first time once.

And the songs you hear when you're young.

They're like nothing else you'll ever hear again.

No matter how banal, how odd, how mediocre, how peculiar, how local they are, they're perfect.

Because they're a mirror of you.

And you're perfect.

If you could but know it.

Holding it now, I can feel you, I can almost touch you.

Young Amy.

And all the things you don't know.

And all the things you do.

And all your dreams.

And fears.

And hopes.

And wishes.

I wish I could touch you.

I wish you could touch me.

It's okay.
It's okay.
It's okay.

She lays the stylus on the vinyl . . .

Five four three two one . . . 'Dive for Your Memory'.

'Dive for Your Memory' by The Go-Betweens.
Amy falls, as if in a swoon . . .
The Kids catch her.
They lift her up and lay her down, carefully, on the banquette.
They put her into the recovery position.
They take her shoes off.
They lay their jackets over her for a blanket.
They put a washing-up bowl beside her in case she needs to be sick.
They put a glass of water next to her head.
They stroke her head.
They kiss her.
She is asleep and safe.
The Kids return to their hidden berths around the caravan.
Emma sits opposite Lance.
A moment.

Emma Have you got any dope?

Lance . . .

Emma I fancy a joint.

Lance Are you sure?

Emma Why wouldn't I be sure?

Lance You're pregnant.

Emma So.

Lance It's quite strong.

Emma Oh, I see, don't worry about that. I actually smoke dope pretty regularly. It's pretty normal in the corporate world. Not before meetings or anything. I even take a bit of coke sometimes. Don't tell my husband.

Lance I won't.

Emma He doesn't approve.

Lance I've got beer if you'd prefer.

Emma I want dope.

Lance Okay.

He starts to make a joint using an album cover as a little platform to roll.

Emma Look at you. Look at you rolling a joint. Licking the papers. Sprinkling tobacco. The sun sparkling on the sea. Sitting in your caravan like a king. Not a care in the world. If I could sketch, you right now, would be the sort of thing I would sketch . . . 'Lance Rolling a Joint' then I'd make it into a watercolour . . .
Frame it, put it up on the wall of the bathroom.
On the wall beside the toilet.
I wouldn't explain it, it would just be there. Always wondering about the story. One day he'd realise what it was.
Teenage friends noticing it when they come round. 'Who's Lance? Did your mum paint that?'

A moment.

Lance?

Lance Mm?

Emma Do you think I'm boring?

Lance No.

Emma It's just, you sort of winced.

Lance Did I?

Emma You did.
When I was talking just then.
Visibly.

Lance I'm sorry.
I'm not really used to company. Sometimes I have friends back. But mostly I'm in here on my own with my DVDs.
I don't know how to be.

Emma Sorry I'm not Tarkovsky.
I could just sit here and look enigmatic if you like?
Cut my wrists.

Lance What?

Emma It's fine. I don't mean anything. I'm joking. I'm just joking. My husband says I have a stupid sense of humour.

Lance Here.

He lights the joint, gives it to her.

Emma Thank you.

She inhales, coughs.
A moment.
She coughs again.

Lance What did you write today?

Emma Today?

Lance Yeah.

Emma This afternoon.
I wrote a scene where Genevieve and the German were hiding in a field.
A field of barley.
Below the town, the town's up on a steep hill, a château at the top.
And the church bells ringing out.
They know the Resistance are looking for them.
And she and he are lying together in amongst the crop.

Facing each other.
At this point in the story, they both know.
But neither of them can admit it.
I tried to imagine what it would be like.
I thought about buzzing insects, and how it would be hot.
And the sound of dogs.
And her being able to hear her own heartbeat.

Lance It sounds good.

Emma Doesn't it?!
The thing is.
When I imagined it.
It was so vivid.
And it felt so true.
And profound.
You know.
But when I started putting it into words.
It just came out like porn.

He laughs.
  She laughs.

Lance Maybe you should write porn.

A moment.

Emma Tell me something about you.

Lance What sort of thing.

Emma Tell me something about when you were a kid.

Lance Back in prehistory.

Emma When you were a little boy.

Lance What do you want to know?

Emma I don't know.
Something.
Anything.
Did you have a pet?

Lance I had a dog.

Emma What was its name?

Lance She was called Boots.

Emma What sort of dog was Boots?

Lance Just some stray. A mongrel. A bit of everything
I suppose. A woman once told me she looked like a whippet
so if anyone ever asked, I said she was a whippet. She had
belonged to a friend of my older brother who needed to
skip town for some reason, and he'd asked my brother to
look after his dog for him, but my brother hadn't got time
to look after a dog so he gave her to me.

Emma You smile when you talk about her.

Lance I loved her.
I had her for about a year. She slept on my bed.
We went everywhere together.
People would give us food.
Old people in the street would buy her treats.
We'd go to the beach and she'd chase sticks into the sea.
We could waste whole days.

Emma What happened to her?

Lance My brother's friend came back.

Emma Poor Boots.

Lance Boots was fine.
I doubt she noticed.
Boots wasn't even her name.
Boots was just the name I called her.
The guy who owned her called her something else.

Emma What did he call her?

Lance Cunt.

Emma Really?

99

Lance Really.

Emma . . .

Lance Apparently he thought it was funny.

Emma That's awful.

Lance Is it?

A moment.

Emma That poor dog.
Running in and out of the sea.
Full of pure love.
Full of pure joy.
And all the time.
Its . . .
Its owner.
The person it loves more than anything.
Wants to call it that.

Lance He didn't think it was a cunt.
He liked the dog.
He just thought it was funny.

Emma That's worse.
It makes me sad to think about it.

Lance Sorry, I shouldn't have told you.

Emma No, it's okay.
I'm glad you did.

Lance Why.

Emma Because now I can see you as a boy.

A moment.
Emma kisses Lance.
He accepts the kiss.
She withdraws for a second, surprised by herself.
A moment.

She kisses him again, he kisses back.
It's intense for a moment.
She withdraws again.
She takes off her skirt.
A moment.

Hold me.

Emma falls, as if in a swoon.
The Kids lift her up.
They carry her to Lance.
They arrange her around him.
They arrange Lance around her.
They arrange them both on the banquette, entwined
around each other, spooned.
They fold Emma's skirt and lay it neatly on the floor.
They take off Emma's shoes and lay them neatly on
the floor.
They close Emma's eyes.
Emma and Lance are asleep and safe.
The Kids withdraw to their berths.

Kids From the perspective of now, describe yourself in a couple of sentences.

— I am awkward. Lots of happy acquaintances, not many friends.

— Class clown, overly thoughtful, curious.

— Emotional, hopeful, dramatic.

— Aggression covers insecurity, lonely, but making no sacrifices to fit in. I will never.

— Romantic, adventurous, excited, free – except if I drink too much vodka, then very emotional and forlorn.

— Juvenile. Good natured. The new kid. A bit lost.

— Awkward, unhinged, uneducated, uncouth, pimply.

— Bursting out, coming into myself but at the same time, bursting.

— Confused. Alive. Conflicted.

— Full of fire.

All the Kids are now asleep, and safe.
Time passes.
Dawn light filters through the caravan window gently illuminating the scene.
Peace.
Emma's phone pings with an incoming message.
Emma's phone pings again with an incoming message.
Emma's phone pings again with an incoming message.
Lance wakes up.

Lance Em.
Em.
Em.

Emma wakes up, groggy.
A moment.

Someone wants you.

Emma It's too bright.

Lance It's nearly ten.

Emma's phone pings again with an incoming message.
Emma's phone pings again with an incoming message.

Someone really wants to get hold of you.

Emma Someone really wants to get hold of *you*!

She cuddles him.
A moment.
She realises she is in her pants and her skirt is folded up.

Lance –
Did we?

Last night?
Did we . . .?

Lance No.

Emma . . .

Lance . . .

Emma Probably for the best.

Lance Probably.

Emma . . .

Lance . . .

She touches his face.

Emma All my borders have gone.
I feel like a teenager.
Soft.
Longing for a boy.
A boy who doesn't even exist.

Amy wakes up.
She takes in the scene.

Amy Emma.

A moment.

Emma Amy.

Amy Why are you in your pants?

A moment.

Lance Shall I make some breakfast for us all.

Suddenly a gunshot.

Emma What the fuck was that!?

Kid A, outside the caravan, shoots the air rifle into the air.

Kid A *Emma! Emma! Get out here, you cow!*

The Kids inside the caravan wake up in fright.

Paedo!

Gasps and screams, as Kid A bursts into the caravan.

Lance Jesus Christ!

Kid A points the air rifle at Emma.

Lance What's going on, [*Kid A*].

Kid A *She kissed* [Kid B].

Emma I don't know what [*s/he's*] talking about.

Kid A *Last night at the dance you kissed* [Kid B]. *Everybody saw.*

Emma Oh.

Amy Emma?

Emma I did it for a bet.

Amy A bet?

Emma [*Kid B*] said it was for a bet!

Amy Jesus Christ, Em.

Emma It didn't mean anything.

Kid A *Don't tell me what means something!*

Emma They said if I kissed them they'd win twenty quid.

Lance [*Kid A*]. Put the gun down.

Amy Who is [*Kid B*] anyway?

Kid B *I am.*

Amy This is who you kissed?

Emma It was for a bet.

Kid A *You've got [him/her]* in here! That's proof!

Kid B *Nothing happened!*

Kid A *Then why are you here in the morning?*

Kid B *Lance had a party.*

Kid A *A party!?*

Kid B *We were just hanging out.*

Kid A *So why wasn't I invited!*

Lance *[Kid A]* . . .

   Lance moves to the Kid with the gun.

Kid A *Don't touch me!*

   Kid A fires in the air.

Emma Fuck!

Kid A *You said you loved me,* [Kid B].

Kid B *I know but –*

Kid A *Behind the caravans, yesterday, we kissed and you said you'd love me forever.*

Kid B *I know, but we're going home tomorrow.*

Kid A *What's that got to do with anything?*

Kid B *The holiday's over.*

Kid A *Are you saying you don't love me?*

Kid B *No!*

Kid A *So, you do love me?*

Kid B *I don't know.*

Kid A *What is it then?*
  Do you love me?
  Or don't you?

Amy I think you'd better answer, love.

Kid A *You keep out of this, witch!*

Kid B *I don't know what I feel,* [Kid A].

Kid A *How can you not know what you feel!?*
You're feeling it!
Just say!

Emma Look, [*Kid A*], I know you're upset but, whatever it is you're feeling now – love, infatuation, hurt – however sore it is, I promise you, I promise, it'll pass.

Amy It won't.

Emma It will.

Amy No, it won't.

Emma Amy.

Amy I'm only telling the truth.

Emma Well, it's not helpful.

Amy For fuck's sake, if there's one thing this weekend has proved, Emma, it's that whatever feelings [*Kid A*] is feeling right now they're going to echo through [*his/her*] universe forever . . .
[*Kid A*]'s going to be thinking about [*Kid B*] when they're fifty-two.
When they're both married with kids.
Dreaming the way life could have been.
There'll still be echoes of this in their lives till they die.
I'm sorry, [*Kid A*], but there's no point sugar-coating it.

Kid A *Shut up, you fucking weirdos.*
Just answer me, [Kid B], *why can't you just answer me?*

Emma Look, [*Kid A*], [*Kid B*] can't possibly be in love you. Not in any real sense. Not in any meaningful sense of that word.

Kid A *Why not?*

Emma Because [*s/he's*] only eighteen and nobody who's eighteen knows anything about anything, especially not about love.

Kid A [S/he's] *sixteen.*

Emma What?

Kid A [Kid B]*'s not eighteen, she's sixteen.*

Emma Oh for fuck's sake, [*Kid B*]!
I could shoot you myself.

Kid A *Paedo!*

> *Kid A shoots.*
> *Lance dives in front of Emma.*

Lance Fuck!

> *Lance falls to his knees.*
> *Kid A drops the gun.*

I'm hit?
I'm hit.
I'm hit.

> *Lance falls to the floor.*

Emma *and* **Amy** Lance!

> *They rush to him.*
> *End of Act Four.*

Act Five

Outside Paradise.
Sunday, mid-morning.
Cool, a sea fog.

Amy and Emma sit on the balconette.
They wear blankets over their shoulders and nurse strong coffees.
Amy pops a painkiller and offers the packet to Emma.
Emma shakes her head.

Emma I prefer to feel it.

Amy What?

Amy lights two cigarettes.

Fag?

Emma Ta.

She gives a cigarette to Emma.
A moment.

Amy When you're young your body's like a harp or something.
The air just moves through it.
I remember just keeping going.
One minute crying, the next just filled with.
I don't know . . .
Whatever it was, if I let those feelings out now, they'd probably burn right through me like the Chernobyl core.
You can take emotion like that that when you're fifteen.
Not now.
All that teenage radioactivity.
You throw up walls around it.
Shut it up in concrete until.

You'd hardly know it was there.
The teenage heart abandoned.
Wolves wandering the car parks.
Wild boar in the mini-mart.
Peace.
Then along comes the past.
And smashes a hole in the sarcophagus.
All safety.
Gone.

Emma reaches out for Amy and holds her hand.

Emma It'll be all right.

Amy Will it?
I used to ask myself –
Will I ever be happy?
Will I ever be right?
Will I ever be understood?
Will I ever be the lead singer in a band?
Will I ever tour in a van?
Will I ever meet Prince?
Well.
I met Prince.

Emma I didn't know you met Prince.

Amy He did a secret late-night gig at the Trocadero when
he was touring in 2005.
I was sleeping with the promoter.

Emma What was he like?

Amy Bit of a dick.

Emma Prince or the promoter?

Amy Both.

A moment.

Did you sleep with Lance last night?

Emma No.

Amy Did you try to?

Emma Yes.

A moment.

Amy Why did you do that, sis?

Emma You got all the lives, Amy, I only got the one.
Everything there was to have, you got it first and you got it twice. You got the boys, the holidays, the adventures, the husbands, the kids, the jobs, the stories, you even got the emotions.
And all the time I pulled along after you . . . in your wake, left with . . . what? I'll tell you what?
Fuck all.

Amy Not quite fuck all.

Emma What do you mean?

Amy You got the happiness, Em.

Emma Oh, fuck happiness.
Everybody's happy.
Cows are happy.
Dogs are happy.
Anyone can be happy.
Last night – for a moment – I wanted to be in the drama.
That's all.

Amy Well, you certainly got that.

Emma I certainly did.

Amy You were lucky to escape alive.

Emma Lance saved me.

Amy You should write about that in your book.

Emma It's not that sort of book.

A moment.

Amy It's probably just as well.

Emma Probably.

Amy It would have complicated your employee relationship with Lance if you'd slept with him.

Emma There won't be an employee relationship.

Amy What!?
You're not going to fire him, are you?
He's a bloody good DJ, Em, you saw that last night.

Emma I'm not going to fire him.

Amy Then what?

Emma Dunnimore will not be buying Holiday Heaven.

Amy Why not?

Emma Gary doesn't like the idea.

Amy So?

Emma It's his company.

Amy But you're a partner.

Emma He ran the numbers.
He called some people he knows.
And he texted me this morning to tell me.
It's not worth it.
The recoverable value in Holiday Heaven is 'negligible'.

Amy Negligible?

Emma You could use the land to build houses.
That's basically it.

Amy But you had a plan.

Emma It's his company.

A moment.

Amy Fucking Gary.

Emma What's that supposed to mean?

Amy He's such an unutterable sap.

Emma He's not a sap.

Amy Oh for God's sake, Emma, he whittles spoons.

Emma I don't think that's sappy.
I think it's actually quite contemplative.
And practical.

Amy Practical?

Emma While he's on phone calls he whittles spoons for the little one.

Amy If you don't stop him, he'll whittle you a papoose.

Emma I don't think that's likely.

Amy He'll probably start whittling his own Lego.

Emma I think that would be quite charming.

Amy You'll have left him in five years.

Emma Amy!

Amy Five years max.
I promise you.
I'm your sister, Em, I've lived through this once myself.
Trust me.
You'll have the baby and it'll all be amazing but soon you'll sink into the great bog of motherhood and you won't know who you are any more, or what you like, or what might make someone over the age of five want to spend time with you, until your whole sense of self turns into a kind of indeterminate rancid mush . . . like an overripe yogurt in the back of the fridge . . . and then one day you'll

be looking out of the window of your lovely apartment over the city, wondering what your name is, and you'll look over to the living-room table and you'll see Gary, on the phone, whittling a spoon.

And that'll be it.

That evening you'll be down the hot-yoga studio putting the moves on Giancarlo.

Emma I don't agree with you.
I don't think that's going to be the story of my life.
I think your experience has left you jaundiced.

Amy I'm sorry.
You're right.
I'm just angry for you.
You had a dream.
And Gary stomped on it.

Emma Buying the campsite was a dumb idea.
Gary put me right.

A moment.

Amy It was a lovely idea.
Childhood.
What's wrong with childhood.

A moment.
A figure slowly emerges out of the mist.

Jesus Christ.

Emma Lance!

Lance Can I sit down.
Please?

Lance has a bandage around his lower torso and upper thigh.
He is walking with a crutch.
Otherwise, he is roughly as we left him the night before.
Perhaps a little greyer.

Emma arranges another chair for him.
He sits.
It hurts.

Emma How are you?

Amy What did the doctors say?

Emma Are you all right?

Lance I'm fine.
It was just a scratch.
Only an air rifle.
No serious damage.
They dug out the pellet.
Gave me some codeine.
Doc says I should be back to normal in a week.

Amy What about [*Kid A*].

Lance I spoke to [*his/her*] mother.
[*S/he's*] a good kid.
It was an accident.
No need to involve the cops.

Emma You were injured.

Lance Her mother brought a cake to the hospital.

Amy A cake?!
You deserve compensation.

Emma I could represent you.

Amy You don't do law.

Emma I *do* law.

Lance Look.
It's fine.
It was a really nice cake.

A moment.

Emma Would you like some coffee.

Lance No thank you.
  I need to sleep.
  It was a big night.

Emma I understand.

  A moment.

Lance Look –
  There's something I want to say.
  This morning, in the hospital.
  I was going over it all round and round in my mind.
  Last night.
  I realised something.
  I realised.
  You coming here.
  You being here this weekend.
  Just when the campsite's being sold.
  It happened for a reason.
  I'm not a religious person.
  But I am spiritual.
  Think there's a meaning behind the mess of the world.
  And last night was a mess.
  But it wasn't meaningless.
  And so.
  I realised.
  This morning.
  And this is what I came here to say –

  A moment.

I want you to stay.

Amy *and* **Emma** What?

Emma Lance?

Amy What are you talking about?

Lance Please.
  I want you to stay.
  With me in the caravan.

Just for a month or so – and then.
When the season's over.
We'll get out.
We'll go.
To Europe.
Buy a cheap camper van.
Throw some stuff in the back.
A mattress, a stove.
Drive somewhere.
Some Italian hill town.
Busk.
Write our own songs.
Visit castles.
Get drunk.
Sit by fires.
Write.
I thought my last chance had gone.
I thought nothing new could ever happen to me.
But since you've been here – I've realised . . .
This is it.
You're my chance.
Stay.
I want you.

A moment.
  A moment.
  A moment.

Amy Lance?

Lance Mmm?

Emma Which one of us are you talking to?

Amy Which one of us do you want to stay, Lance?

Lance Oh . . .
  I'm sorry.
  Sorry, was it not clear?

Amy It wasn't clear, no.

Lance Oh Christ.
Sorry, I'm not good at this.
I knew I should have practised.

Emma Which one of us are you talking to?

A moment.

Lance Amy.

A moment.

Emma I'll leave you to it.

Amy Emma.

Emma It's fine.

Emma goes inside the caravan and shuts the door hard behind her.

Lance I'm sorry.

Amy It's all right.

Lance I never thought she'd think . . .

Amy No.

A moment.

Lance So, what do you say?

Amy No.

Lance No?

Amy No, Lance.
I don't want to leave my husband and kids and go backpacking round Europe with you and an acoustic guitar.

Lance Oh.

Amy It's very nice of you to ask, honestly, it really is.
I mean that.
But our ship sailed a long, long time ago.

Lance But last night –

Amy Last night I agreed with you last night when you said we were inevitably going to fuck.

For what it's worth, I still think that might be true.

But I have a life, Lance. I might be terrible at it. I might be unhappy. But the life I have is the one I've made and I can't go about un-making it. Not just like that.

I'm not like you, Lance, I am entangled.

And if I were to decide to untangle myself.

It would only be to be alone.

So.

Thank you very much for asking, Lance.

But no.

And may I have your mobile number because . . . well because . . .

If there isn't forever, there's always tonight.

Lance Sorry, Ames.

Doc says I shouldn't strain my groin, not till it's properly healed.

Amy Fair enough.

Lance Fair enough.

Amy Are you heartbroken?

Lance A bit.

Amy But not enough to try one more time to persuade me?

Lance Is there any chance of you changing your mind?

Amy No.

Lance Oh well.

I'm pretty relieved, to be honest.

When I was lying there, this morning, in the hospital bed, I felt pretty scared. If you'd actually said 'yes', I didn't know what I'd have done.

A moment.

Amy Why didn't you come to the city, Lance?

A moment.

Lance You were always a star, Amy.
Even then.
You could sing, and write and think and talk and . . .
– You radiate – you still do.
I play records, I can't make them.
You were miles out of my league.
I didn't want to drag you down.

Amy I loved you.

Lance You loved my records.
And one day you were bound to find out that you could get those on your own.

Amy Did you get my letters.

Lance All of them.

Amy Why didn't you reply?

Lance I kept meaning to but –

Amy But what?

Lance Writing's hard.

A moment.

Amy I forgot about you pretty quickly.

Lance . . .

Amy I mean I was furious at first, of course, I raged, and pined.
But by Christmas I'd started going out with a guy called Gregory who played bass. He looked like Michael Hutchence, if Michael Hutchence had been Irish. We formed a band. It was pretty wild.

Lance You were in a band?

Amy I was in a few.

Lance Oh.
  Would I know any of them?

Amy Crazed Bitch? The Dirty Ballgowns? Nine-Mile Hike? Urban Fox?
  Amy and the Emendations?

Lance No.

Amy Nothing happened.
  Despite your certainty, Lance.
  I may radiate but.
  I appear not to radiate anything the public actually wants.

  A moment.

Lance I was so sure I'd see you on TV one day. Hear you on the radio. For years I'd lie awake at night and wonder – were you looking at the same moon? Were you on the same continent? Was someone lying beside you?
  After a while I thought maybe you'd found religion and become, you know, a nun or something.

Amy Me – a nun?

Lance I know.
  Another time I imagined you'd run away and gone backpacking round Asia.

Amy I did do that for a while.

Lance Another time I imagined you'd ended up in the suburbs with two big Alsatians and a lesbian.

Amy I did that for a while too.
  No Alsatians.

Lance Then one day I took all the feelings, all the things I wanted to say, and I wrote them down in a letter to you, I addressed it to your old address, stamped it.
  Put it in a bottle.
  Threw it into the sea.

A moment.
A moment.
A moment.
She goes over to him.
She kisses him.
He kisses her back.
Amy and Lance wrap themselves around each other
like a pair of teenagers . . .
The Kids emerge from the mist.

Kids You, aged sixteen, can ask your older self a question about the future, and your older self must answer truthfully. What question would you like to ask?

— Is it like *Back to the Future?*
A little bit, just no hoverboards.

— Where do I live?
In another country.

— Are you and your family happy and safe?
Yes. You can relax.

— Will I become successful?
Yes, but your definition of success changes as you go through life.

— What will happen to me?
It will turn out great. The fear, confusion and self-loathing will stop. Sort of.

— Will I survive this year?
Yes, but it will scar. It'll be as hard in retrospect as it is right now.

— Are you happy?
Yes, very.

— Will I have a boyfriend?
Yes. And no.

— Will I marry Kristian?
No.

— Will my brother be okay?
Yes, more than you could imagine.

— Will it hurt?
Yes it will.

— Will you still know Shane?
Distantly.

— Will you still have these friends?
Yes, closer than ever. You still see them.

— Will you get to be an actor, will my dream come true?
Yes.

— Do I feel better?
Yes.

— Do I have a partner?
Yes.

— Do I make it?
Yes.

— Will I be loved by someone?
Yes, but you are going to have to wait a long time, longer than most.

— Will I be famous?
No, but you will have realised that wasn't what you wanted anyway.

— Where will I live?
It will take a while, but you will move out of that small town and finally find your place in the city and everything will begin falling into place.

> *. . . Finally, Amy breaks away from Lance . . . happy, breathless.*

Amy Go.
Go.

Lance goes.
A moment.
Emma comes out.

Emma Where's Lance?

Amy He's gone.

Emma Aren't you going to go with him?

Amy No.

Emma Why not?

Amy It's not that sort of novel.

A moment.

Emma So, what are you going to do?

Amy I thought maybe I could stay with you.
Just till I get my head together.

Emma I'm on retreat, Amy.

Amy I'll be as quiet as a mouse, I promise.

Emma I'm trying to write.

Amy Please.

A moment.

Emma All right.

Amy You're a life-saver.

Emma I'm a fucking enabler is what I am.
At least text Dan, let him know you're alive.

Once more, the two of them sit together on the
balconette.
Emma puts her sunglasses on.

She takes out her notebook.
A moment.
She writes something down.
A moment.
Amy gets out her phone.
A moment.

Amy I'm okay. Need space. Broken heart.

A moment.
She holds her phone up to the Kids . . .

'Emma and Amy are still here' . . . Five four three two one . . .

She presses play: The Kids' song.

The End.